You don't have to be Jewish to love this book....
But it wouldn't hurt.

✡ ✡ ✡

Was Elvis Jewish? That's not all this book will tell you. There's something for everyone here, including the religious and the irreverent, the young and the not-so-young. Most of the information will be unknown to you. It's been scattered and often lost in various and hard-to-find newspaper stories, websites, and books. But now these anecdotes, facts, jokes, lists, and pieces of history and commentary—both heavy and light—are in one very readable and riveting volume. *This one.*

Discover what you didn't know about Jewish-related movies, shows, TV, comedians, celebrities, history, royalty, politics, tradition, kosher food and wine, sports, holidays & holy days, pets, dating, prejudice, Palestinians, books, boycotts, Yiddish, Israeli innovations & inventions, Israeli life, travel, health, websites, and more.

You'll read all about ashpoopie, bagels, baseball, BDS, Bibles, Borscht Belt, boxing, Brando, Casablanca, Chabad, Chai Technology, chicken soup, Chinese food, Christmas, circumcision, the Clintons, Billy Crystal, Dirty Dancing, Downton Abbey, dreidels, Everybody Loves Raymond, Fiddler on the Roof, Anne Frank, gefilte fish, Hanukkah, Harry Potter, Hebrew, Hitler, IDF (Israel Defense Forces), Israel, kosher marijuana, "Magic" Yarmulkas, Mikvahmobiles, Olympics, online dating, Passover, Rabbis, Joan Rivers, (Dr.) Ruth, Sabbath, Schindler's List, Seders, Seinfeld, shiksas, skunk spray, soldiers, Frank Sinatra, Starbucks, startups, Jon Stewart, Star Wars, Yinglish, Yom Kippur, and much more.

So get started!

WAS
ELVIS
JEWISH?

Plus Hundreds Of Other
Amazing & Amusing
Anecdotes
No Rabbi Ever Told You

Paulette Cooper

WAS ELVIS JEWISH?
Plus Hundreds of Other
Amazing & Amusing Anecdotes
No Rabbi Ever Told You

Published by PoloPublishing of Palm Beach
PO Box 621, Palm Beach, FL 33480

SBN-13: 978-0991401369

For more copies of this book go to www.waselvisjewish.com
To reach the author, email polopublishing@aol.com

Credits: Graphic Design by Mia Crews. Elvis cover cartoon by Ron Leischman. Siley cartoon designed for the book by TargetJump. Front cover cartoons: © Can Stock Photo Inc./ cthomas; ©Can Stock Photo Inc./dedMazay. Back ©Can Stock Photo Inc./caraman. Photo of author: courtesy of Tina Valant

ACKNOWLEDGMENTS

I want to thank Mia Crews for the layout and design. I want to thank Albert Podell, who stole time from working on his bestseller *Around the World in 50 Years,* to advise me and go over this manuscript.

I also want to thank Rob Clark, along with my late great friend, Tania Grossinger, for her suggestions and encouragement.

Thanks also to my genius flexagonal friend, Ann Schwartz, who edited and improved my back cover copy and front matter. (Not to mention her terrific cat Leica for her unsolicited opinions on everything.)

And finally, to my wonderful husband for his editing, encouragement, and love.

DEDICATION

To that "nice Jewish boy" I finally made my mother (and myself) happy by marrying, Paul Noble.

TABLE OF CONTENTS

INTRODUCTION

Once, I would have been the last person in the world to write anything "Jewish." My parents were killed in Auschwitz and I wanted nothing to do with what caused that. I also felt overly exposed to my Judaism. My adopted parents were religious. I was brought up in a kosher home (craving lobster and bacon) and I went to Brandeis (which served neither).

So I turned to other topics. The first book I wrote, *The Scandal of Scientology,* was about this powerful fascistic cult. I also wrote about forensic medicine, *The Medical Detectives,* which was the first book on the subject for the layman, later popularized by CSI. In Palm Beach, where I live, I also write a newspaper column titled "Pet Set," reflecting another great interest of mine, dogs, and cats. Six of my 23 books have been on that subject.

But two years ago I happened upon some interesting light stories and facts about Jews and Judaism. I saw what a fascinating—yes, even fun—subject it could be. The more I learned as I researched this book, the more interested I became in my background, which I had once turned away from.

I put this book together for me as well as for you, carefully choosing topics and jokes that would be engrossing and enjoyable even for the non-religious non-identifying Jew as well as for the Gentile.

Writing this book made me much more interested in my heritage and proud to be a Jew. I hope it has the same effect on my fellow Jews and inspires friendship from all.

Paulette Cooper (Noble)

CHAPTER 1
WHO'S A JEW? WHO KNEW?

SORT-OF ROYAL

WAS ELVIS ("THE KING") JEWISH? Now hopefully this will not get you all shook up, but it seems that **Elvis Presley's** mother's maternal grandmother named **Martha (Burdine) Tackett** was probably Jewish. That doesn't mean "Elvis has left the building" would ever have become "Elvis is on his way to the synagogue," but not only was he sort-of Jewish by matrilineal descent, he was Jewish in ways most people don't know.

He knew it, though, and Elvis's Jewish heritage seems to have spoken to him in some way since he wore a *Chai* symbol, meaning life, on his necklace. He often paired this with a cross, which he wore at the same time. Indeed, when the King was found dead on the "throne,"and yes, he died on the toilet, he was wearing that very Chai necklace. When asked why he wore a Jewish symbol, he never mentioned his Jewish ancestry. Instead, he was often quoted as saying: "I don't want to be kept out of heaven on a technicality."

Now grab your blue suede shoes because there's more. His mother's gravestone. When Elvis's mother, **Gladys,** who wanted Elvis to be a doctor, not a singer, was buried at Forest Hill Cemetery, Elvis's father had a Christian cross put on her gravestone. That's no surprise. But around 1970, Elvis designed a *new* headstone, which included a Star of David, along with the cross, in honor of her Jewish heritage. Alas, when her body was moved from the original cemetery to Graceland, the Jewish star on the new gravestone was omitted. Accident? Yeah, sure. But his Chai necklace remains on display in a glass case, although there's no explanation surrounding it.

Strangely enough, when Elvis was young, just a Prince, not yet a King, he was a shabbos goy (Christian who performs tasks forbidden for Jews to perform on the Sabbath) for a rabbi who lived upstairs. *Shmelvis: In Search of Elvis Presley's Jewish Roots* tracked down the rabbi's widow, **Jeanette Fruchter.** She recalled that Elvis called her husband "Sir Rabbi" and would come over every Saturday morning, turn the lights on, and do other goyishe things that needed doing. Although they offered him a tip, and his early poverty was legendary, they said he never accepted it.

Elvis did accept—and loved—their matzo ball soup and challah, which he ate at their monthly Friday night Shabbat dinner to which he was a frequent guest. Years later, it was often reported that he spread his peanut butter and banana concoction on challah. The Rebbetzin also said that Elvis carried a yarmulke in his pocket and presumably wore it at their Shabbat dinners, and hopefully not when he was doing his shabbos goy gigs

The authors of *Shmelvis...*, **Jonathan Goldstein,** and **Max Wallace,** traveling around on what they called their "Winnebagel," also tracked down Elvis's former (Jewish) landlady. She said of "Elvis'l," as her family called him: "When I first knew him he had a big nose and not such beautiful skin. But after his [nose] surgery, he turned into a very fine looking young man."

The King also bestowed some large pieces of gold to Jewish charities in a probable homage to his roots. A famous story concerns the Memphis Jewish Welfare organization. Elvis was known to give most charities that asked for money $1,000. Instead, he gave them $150,000—the equivalent of more than a million dollars today!

If you're still uncertain whether Elvis was (sort of) Jewish, here's definitive proof:

- He loved matzo ball soup;
- His mother wanted him to be a doctor;
- He loved Cadillacs.
- He had a nose job.

Convinced?

☺ PROOF THAT JESUS WAS JEWISH

- He went into His Father's business.
- He lived at home until He was 33.
- He was sure His Mother was a virgin.
- His Mother was sure He was God.

SORT-OF JEWISH

SECRETARY OF STATE JOHN KERRY'S FAMILY WERE THE (JEWISH) KOHNS How did the Jewish Kohns become the Irish Kerrys? When Kerry's Jewish great-grandfather, living in what is now Czechoslovakia, decided to come to America, the family reinvented themselves. One dropped a pencil on a map, which landed on Ireland's Kerry County. Bingo, their new nationality—and name.

Incredibly, **John Kerry** claimed not to know about his Jewish roots. He naively—and unconvincingly—claimed he didn't know about his background until 2003 when he supposedly learned it from a *Boston Globe* article. Yeah, sure. Someone once said that if someone wants to find out if they have Jewish roots, they should simply run for President.

Lisa Katz, writing about Kerry's Jewish relatives in *about.com* said bluntly that this Secretary of State and practicing Irish Catholic, who was almost President of the United States, was Jewish enough that if his past had come out during the Nazi era, he would have been sent to a concentration camp. [Note: the Nazis used grandparents, not great-grandparents as the determinant, so this is a gray area.]

OK, here's the background. The second wife of John Kerry's great-grandfather was a widow named **Mathilde Frankel Kohn.** They had two children, and because of the anti-Semitism rampant in Europe at the time, her two boys converted to Roman Catholicism.

The brother, **Fred,** married **Ida Loewe,** a Jewish musician, two of whose siblings were killed in Nazi concentration camps. Meanwhile, Fred, Ida, and their first son were all baptized as Catholics. In 1905, they came to America.

Fred Kerry, Kerry's grandfather—who, incidentally shot himself in the head when he was 48—ended up in Boston. Fred's son, John Kerry's father, was six and later married **Rosemary Forbes.** She of the fabulously wealthy Forbes family trusts. They had four children. Yep, that good "Catholic" Senator and 2004 Democratic Nominee for President was one of them. Another one of the sons, **Cameron,** married a Jew and converted to Judaism.

When Kerry was trying to negotiate peace between Israel and the Palestinians, could there have been any relationship between John Kerry's attempt to hide his background and then blaming Israel for the failure of some peace talks? And then outrageously and erroneously accusing Israel of being an apartheid state?

Or is Kerry simply clueless? As **Daniel Greenfield** said, as if speaking to Kerry in an article in the *JewishPress.com:* "When did you [Kerry] successfully negotiate anything, up to and including the purchase of your latest yacht?"

WAS HARRY POTTER JEWISH? *Jewornotjew.com,* which rates stars on their Jewishness, says that the movie character of Harry isn't Jewish because "He goes to Hogwarts, not a yeshiva, wears a Gryffindor scarf, not a tallis, drinks pumpkin juice, not Manischewitz, etc."

But the 5' 5" tall **Daniel Radcliffe,** who plays Harry Potter, has a Jewish mother and Protestant father. And he describes himself as proud of being Jewish.

Here's three more little-known facts about him, two of them odd, one of them enviable:

- He can rotate his arm 360 degrees.
- He believes in magic.
- He has made 6 million pounds from his movies, making him the second richest young person in Britain, after Prince Harry. Windsor.

THANK GOD FOR JEWS

YOU WOULDN'T HAVE KNOWN THESE IF NOT FOR JEWS
Barbie dolls, blue jeans (Levis), remote control, Vinyl (disc) records, Valium, Q-tips, Sweet'n Low, Esperanto, flexible straws, birth control pills, holography, Polaroid, the Lincoln penny (the design was done by a Jew), maternity bras, standardized bra cup sizes (A,B,C, etc.)

AND YOU WOULDN'T HAVE KNOWN WHAT TO EXPECT
Pregnant women wouldn't have known what to expect if not for the wildly successful *What to Expect When You're Expecting*. It was written by journalist **Arlene Eisenberg**, along with her (and journalist **Howard Eisenberg's)** two daughters, **Heidi Murkoff,** and nurse **Sandee Hathway**.

WHAT WOULD SHOPPING HAVE BEEN LIKE IF NOT FOR THESE? Craigslist, barcodes, department stores, mail order catalogs, shopping carts, drug stores, and infomercials. Better the last hadn't been invented!)

WHAT WOULD WOMEN HAVE LOOKED LIKE IF NOT FOR MAKSYMILIAN FAKTOROWICZ? You know, Max Factor. No nail polish, no French manicures, no lip gloss, no smear-proof lipstick, no concealer, no waterproof makeup, no colorless mascara, no long-lasting lipstick, no false eyelashes, no make-up foundation.

NAME THAT JEW!

Actress Natalie Portman was Natalie Herschlag.

Joaquin Phoenix (mother Jewish; father Catholic) was actually Joaquin Bottom, and at one point called himself Leaf Phoenix and has a sister named Rain.

Albert Brooks was Albert Einstein.

Judge Judy (Sheindlin) was Judith Blum.

Gene Simmons, the bass player for the rock band, "KISS," was named Chaim Witz.

Ayn Rand, the controversial author, was Alissa Rosenbaum.

Dyan Cannon, an actress, is Samile Diane Friesen.

Larry King was Lawrence Zeiger.

Heywood Allen, at 17, Woody Allen changed his name from Allan Konigsberg to Heywood Allen, called "Woody."

"Dr. Ruth" Westheimer was Karola Siegel.

Harry Houdini, the famous illusionist and stunt artist, escaped from his own name, Erich Weiss.

SO NU-ISH?
THEY'RE NOT REALLY JEWISH

FAMOUS KILLERS WE'RE GLAD WEREN'T JEWISH. OR WERE THEY? The minute you hear or read about someone doing something terrible, don't you immediately start hoping, even praying, that they aren't Jewish? Here are some people who happily were **not.**

OJ SIMPSON Bad enough he killed his wife, let's not forget that he also slaughtered that nice Jewish boy, **Ronald Goldman**.

DAVID "SON OF SAM" BERKOWITZ One of America's most notorious serial killers, he terrorized New York over a one-year period. He killed six people and wounded seven more, mostly long-haired women sitting in cars. Born to Jewish parents, he was adopted and brought up by non-Jews. *Whew.*

LEE HARVEY OSWALD Presumed assassin of **President Kennedy**, he had a prototypically overbearing Jewish mother—who happily was not Jewish. Nor was his father. But *his* killer, **Jack Ruby**—that's another (awful) story.

GEORGE ZIMMERMAN The self-styled vigilante accused of killing **Trayvon Martin**, an unarmed African American in Florida, is not at all Jewish.

JOHN WILKES BOOTH Oy, **President Lincoln's** famous assassin may have been of Spanish Jewish descent, according to *Abraham Lincoln's Great Gift to the Jews*. Both Booth's sister and brother claimed that their father, **Junius Brutus Booth,** was Jewish.

IS HALF A JEW BETTER THAN NONE?

RAIDERS OF THE LOST TEMPLE Harrison Ford (*Raiders of the Lost Ark, Indiana Jones,* etc.) had a mother, **Dora Nidelman,** who was 100% Jewish. Ford's father was Irish, and Ford says he feels "Irish as a person but Jewish as an actor."

NOT JUST A PRETTY PUNIM Marilyn Monroe, after she married playwright **Arthur Miller,** became one of Judaism's most famous converts of her time. Marilyn said that she was aware of the great characters that the Jewish people had produced—and that she had read selections from **Albert Einstein's** *Out of My Later Years*. Apparently, she thought that qualified her.

BUDDHIST JEW Kate Hudson is of Italian, English, and Hungarian Jewish descent. She was raised in her maternal grandmother's Jewish religion, but her family also practiced Buddhism. Her mother is actress/comedian **Goldie Hawn,** perhaps best known for the old TV series *Laugh-In*.

A FRIEND Lisa Kudrow is not only a "Friend" but also a Jewish friend, since she was raised in an Eastern European background. On the show, *Who Do You Think You Are?* which helps celebrities learn their genealogies, she discovered that her paternal great-great-grandmother had been murdered during the Holocaust.

A FEW WELL-KNOWN PEOPLE WHOSE FATHERS WERE JEWISH Writer **Joan Collins**, Actress **Jamie Lee Curtis,** EST cult leader **Werner Erhard** (born **John Paul Rosenberg**), Actress and writer **Carrie Fisher** (her mother was actress **Debbie Reynolds;** her father was actor and singer **Eddie Fisher**), TV actress **Kathie Lee Gifford,** Actor **Kevin Kline**, Actor **Paul Newman**, Publisher **Joseph Pulitzer**, Actress **Jane Seymour**, TV host **Matt Lauer.**

IF YOU THINK THEY'RE JEWISH…YOU'RE WRONG Julia **Louis-Dreyfus** may have been Jewish on *Seinfeld,* but she does not identify with members of the tribe in real life. Although her father is Jewish—indeed, she's distantly related to **Alfred Dreyfus**, the Jewish French army officer who was unfairly scapegoated—but she was raised Protestant. Indeed, she often wears a cross, probably just so no one should get the wrong idea after Seinfeld.

Jason Biggs played a Jew, Jim Levinson, in the *American Pie* films, plus Larry Bloom in *Orange is the New Black.* So how much more Jewish can you get? But he's Italian and Catholic. Still, he admits that he looks Jewish, so much so that his tagline is "The Jewiest Looking Non-Jew." Apparently, his *dog* is Jewish, though, since Jason had a Bark-Mitzvah for him. Funny, the dog doesn't look Jewish.

Seth Meyers From his name and face, but…he's not Jewish. His paternal grandfather and his wife are another matter. *Popjewish.com* quoted him as saying that his parents-in-law were disappointed when he was dating their daughter and they found out the truth. "How could a Seth Meyers not be Jewish?" they asked themselves as they probably tore their Saks Fifth Avenue garments and sat Shiva.

Meyers said he doesn't like to tell people he's not Jewish because it makes him sound like he's trying to get into a restricted country club.

Director **Norman Jewison** People erroneously assume he's Jewish, not only because of his name but because he directed the movie version of the uber-Jewish show, *Fiddler on the Roof.*

"Weird Al" Yankovic sings a song, "Pretty Fly (For A Rabbi)" but he's not a rabbi, nor is he Jewish.

SURPRISE! THESE STARS NAMES SOUND JEWISH BUT THEY'RE NOT MEMBERS OF THE TRIBE Steve Allen, Justin Bieber, Julius Caesar, Whoopi Goldberg, Barry Goldwater, Phillip Seymour Hoffman, Calvin Klein, Bruce Springsteen, Ringo Starr,

John Steinbeck, George Steinbrenner, Mark Wahlberg, Efrem Zimbalist Jr.

EVEN THEIR MOTHERS THINK THEY'RE JEWISH

Sometimes even their mothers get it wrong. Comedian **Joy Behar** jokes that because of her name, everyone thinks she's Jewish.

She quipped: "Last year I got a call from my mother wishing me a Happy Hanukkah.

"I said: 'Mom, I'm not Jewish.'"

THEY'RE [MOSTLY] JEWISH

SOME PEOPLE WE'RE SORRY ARE "LANDSMEN" [Fellow Jews]

SHIA LaBEOUF Accused of plagiarism; taken to occasionally 1wearing a bag over his head; chasing a homeless man in Times Square to try to take the McDonald's hamburger in his hand, etc. With a name like his, you wouldn't think...you'd be wrong.

BOBBY FISCHER Born to a Jewish mother, some say he was the greatest chess player of all time. But this genius violently and virulently turned against Jews when he became a member of a messianic cult.

DONALD STERLING Former owner of the Clippers, after being caught making racist remarks, was ordered to give up the team.

WYNONA RIDER This half-Jewish actress was a source of pride until she was caught shoplifting. At least she stole from Saks, practically *mishpocha*. How embarrassing would it have been if it had been Walmart or J.C. Penney?

PAULA ABDUL While she's certainly not that bad all the time, this singer, actress and choreographer "reminds us all of that one weird aunt that we sit next to at the Passover Seder," quipped a blogger in *virtualjerusalem.com*.

BERNIE MADOFF There's perhaps a bit of good news about this bad news Ponzi-putz. Once, just about everyone knew who this perpetrator of a 65-billion-dollar scam was, *and* that America's most notorious crook was Jewish. But a decade later, when a survey of college-educated kids from 18 to 29—who invested in the stock market!—found, incredibly, that 25% of them didn't know who Bernie Madoff was! Good.

THE JEW TURNED DOWN BY A COUNTRY CLUB— BECAUSE THEY THOUGHT HE WAS TOO ITALIAN! James Caan was born in the Bronx, the son of Jewish refugees from Germany, **Sophie** and **Arthur Caan**, a meat dealer. Caan is best known for his role as the hotheaded Sonny Corleone in *The Godfather*. Indeed, he was so convincing as an "Italian Stallion" that he won "Italian of the Year" twice in New York.

Weirder still, he was denied membership in a country club—and for a change, it wasn't because they thought the applicant was Jewish. *Jewage.org* quoted him as saying, "The guy sat in front of the board, and he says, 'No, no, he's a wise guy, been downtown. He's a made guy.' I thought, 'What? Are you out of your mind?'"

WHAT DOES A HALF JEW DO?

A famous story, with several variations, concerned a country club that supposedly offered to waive its no-Jews rule for old-time comedian Groucho Marx. But the condition for him to become a member was that he could only join if he didn't use the swimming pool.Groucho supposedly said: "My daughter's only half Jewish. Can she wade in up to her knees?"

IF ANYONE WAS LEFT OUT "It's true-ish, they're Jewish" was the title of an amusing article written by **Emily Stone** that appeared on the website of the Jewish Book Council. Here are a few of the people she wrote about:

Julio Iglesias "True-ish." His mother is Jewish, and he proclaims he is "Jewish from the waist up."

Roseanne Barr True. This presidential nominee and "domestic goddess" is a Jewess through and through.

David Arquette He was born on a Buddhist commune in Virginia to a Jewish mother and a gentile father who converted to Islam... and his family celebrates both Passover and Ramadan.

Sandra Bullock "False-ish." Although "Bullock herself hired a mohel to circumcise her adopted son—wha...?"

Seth Rogen True. "This schlepper's parents met on a kibbutz!"

Goldie Hawn True. Hawn's a practicing Bu-Jew and an avid supporter of Israel.

Tori Spelling True. "All the nose jobs in the world can't hide the fact that Donna Martin's a Jew!"

Jon Hamm "False. Hamm ain't kosher."

WHY DO WE CARE IF SOMEONE'S A JEW? Let's face it, we do care. **Alex Ryvchin**, writing in *Jewishthinker.org,* says perhaps knowing someone is also Jewish "makes us feel a closeness, a sense of community with people with whom we have no other connection. We may have more in common with a Himalayan concubine than the **Baron de Rothschild**, but we still take pleasure in knowing that he is a Jew, and, therefore, share a common history and perhaps a common destiny."

Or maybe it's as simple as pride. "Pride in knowing that a people which account for roughly 0.002% of the world's population have contributed 30% of Nobel prize winners in literature, physics, chemistry and medicine in the last 50 years; produced the quintessential geniuses in **Einstein** and **Freud; the Guggenheims**, the **Marx Brothers**, the **Stooges**, **Spielberg**, and **Seinfeld**; and have even produced a capable sportsman or two—**Mark Spitz.**

"Let's just enjoy learning that **Gwyneth Paltrow** is descended from a long line of rabbis, **David Beckham's** grandfather was Jewish, and **Sylvester Stallone's** grandmother was a Jew from Odessa. And what's the harm in a little Jew-spotting anyway?" he wrote.

JEWS IN HISTORY

WAS JACK THE RIPPER REALLY A JEW? Was Jack the Ripper, the notorious Victorian English serial killer actually a mentally disturbed Jewish barber? To read the British papers, which never miss a chance to say something negative about Jews, the 125⁺-year-old mystery was *definitely* solved in 2014. Indeed, they even mentioned that another earlier candidate had also been a Jew, although if the case was finally closed, what difference does that make?

But was it really solved? The author of a new book, *Naming Jack the Ripper,* **Russell Edwards,** claimed to have used DNA from a shawl he purchased that supposedly came from the Ripper's 4th victim. Working with a molecular biologist, he said that the match was to a 23-year-old Jewish Polish *émigré* paranoid schizophrenic who died in a lunatic asylum. But this **Aaron Kosminski** has always been considered one of the possible Rippers, so that's not new.

But is what's new true? *Thedailybeast.com* summarized the questions raised by the skeptics: "Everything from the shawl's provenance (never clearly established), its true age (possibly manufactured a decade or more after the Ripper murders), and the DNA science used to link the shawl to both the victim and the perpetrator."

As for the DNA: "Due to the degeneration of the genetic material...[they were] forced to rely on less accurate mitochondrial DNA, which American courts have generally ruled is inadmissible in criminal proceedings because it is not a unique identifier." It belongs to a common subgroup that could potentially have come from thousands of people.

Author **Dane Ladwig** wrote a book espousing his theory that **H.H. Holmes** (aka **Herman Mudgett,** the killer in the best-seller *The Devil in the White City*) who killed 30 people, was the real Ripper. He's confident that it couldn't have been Kosminski—mainly because he spoke only Yiddish, not English, and the taunting letters to the police were in English. In addition: "Kosminski was a barber by trade with no refined education in human anatomy [as the real ripper obviously had]. His tool of trade was a barber's shaving razor, not a surgical tool." So, it's pretty easy to rip apart the latest Ripper theory.

CHAPTER 2

THAT'S ENTERTAINMENT
MOVIES & THEIR STARS

STEPHEN SPIELBERG

STEVEN SPIELBERG'S FIRST MAJOR MOVIE, *JAWS*, WAS ALMOST HIS LAST While many think the movie *Jaws* was great, the filming of it was not. *Jaws* was the first major movie directed by **Steven Spielberg**, and the filming went so badly that the crew took to calling the movie "Flaws." And thought of him as "Finished."

According to *Hollywood Stories: Short Entertaining Anecdotes about the Stars and Legends of the Movies,* author **Stephen Schochet** says most of the problems revolved around the 30-foot shark. Called "Bruce" after Spielberg's lawyer, Schocket called the shark "fake-looking... and a new low in ridiculousness."

But Spielberg and the crew also had problems with *real* sharks. They needed one for a shot, but when days went by without a bite, they had to have a frozen tiger shark shipped from Florida. Then they hung the "stinky beast" up for days while the shooting went into overtime. The locals in Martha's Vineyard were so angry they somehow caught some real sharks and threw the smelly dead ones onto the porches of the rented houses of the cast and crew.

A major cause of the problems was that Spielberg refused to use a water tank. But real water presented problems with tides, surf, winds, jellyfish, sharks, waterspouts, hurricane warnings—and local people. The fisherman would sail into the camera range, resulting in long waits, reshot scenes, and new locations. The famous Martha's Vineyard fog also often prevented filming, and in the end, the 10-week shooting took 6 months and cost $10 million dollars.

Spielberg thought that was the end of his career. But then he went to a *Jaws* preview. Eighteen minutes in, when the shark bit a swimmer and blood flowed, someone in the theater ran to the men's room. Spielberg, who was nervously waiting in the lobby, followed him in, watched him throw up–and then return to the movie.

Spielberg knew then that he had a hit.

SPIELBERG AND ANTI-SEMITISM Spielberg was brought up in Haddon Heights, New Jersey, which didn't even allow Jews before World War II. And they weren't very welcome by the time he got there.

So it was probably a great moment for him when he received the Federal Cross of Merit, presented to him by the President, in recognition of *Schindler's List* and his Shoah Foundation, which recorded the history of Holocaust victims. Especially since that Federal Cross was a German award—given to him by the President of Germany.

FASCINATING LITTLE-KNOWN FACTS ABOUT SPIELBERG AND HIS MOVIES Spielberg's first movie? You never saw it. As a child, he took his Lionel train sets, destroyed them, and filmed the destruction in 8mm adventure films. He charged a quarter for admission, and his sister sold popcorn.

He probably made less money on his first real film, which you also didn't see. At 16, he wrote and directed a 2-hour-plus science fiction adventure that might have inspired his later *Close Encounters*. The budget was $500. It played briefly, *very* briefly, in his local cinema. His profit was $1. Today, the unadjusted gross of all Spielberg-directed films exceeds $8.5 billion worldwide.

Don't write a prenup on a napkin. *Forbes* put Spielberg's wealth at $3.0 billion, but it would probably have been 3 billion, 100 million if he had written his prenup on real paper. He had to pay his first wife, actress **Amy Irving,** $100 million after a judge vacated his prenup—which had been written on a napkin.

Although he gave up on that marriage, he generally doesn't give up easily. When young, he applied to the film school at USC School of Theater, Film and Television—and can you imagine?—the idiots turned him down. That didn't stop him from trying two more times—and being turned down each time.

Spielberg didn't finish college, but here too he persisted. More than 30 years later, in 2002, he finally graduated via independent projects. His student film requirement was a 12-minute film. He submitted *Schindler's List*. Think he passed?

Spielberg took no money for *Schindler's List*.

Spielberg is a knight. He was granted an honorary knighthood by **Queen Elizabeth II** in 2001. Although he can use KBE, ("Knight of the British Empire") after his name, he can't be called "Sir Steven Spielberg" because he's not a British citizen.

SPIELBERG 1—KUBRICK 0

Stanley Kubrick, director of *Dr. Strangelove, A Clockwork Orange* and *2001: A Space Odyssey,* was known to some as a self-hating Jew, who was widely quoted as saying that "**Hitler** was right about almost everything."

Kubrick was supposedly a friend of Spielberg's, but one wonders if there wasn't a bit of professional jealousy on the part of Kubrick. According to *Eyes Wide Open: A Memoir of Stanley Kubrick,* Kubrick said that "The Holocaust is about six million people who get killed. *Schindler's List* was about six hundred people who don't."

Those in the film industry found him impossible to work with. He filmed a scene many *many* times. In *Eyes Wide Shut*, he filmed 95 takes of **Tom Cruise** just walking through a door.

"JEWISH" MOVIES—SORT OF

WAS *DIRTY DANCING A* "JEWISH MOVIE"? The writer and co-producer said it was "so Jewish that none of the characters ever need to explicitly mention their Jewishness...It's a Jewish film if you know what you're looking at," *Tabletmag.com* quoted.

What you're looking at is America's seventh most favorite movie according to a recent Harris Poll, what the *BBC* called "Star Wars for Girls," and *The New York Times* called a "Yiddish-inflected Camelot." You're also looking at a low-budget movie that almost didn't make it—because the stars hated each other.

Forget that memorable on-screen sizzling chemistry between **Jennifer Grey** (daughter of **Joel Grey** of *Cabaret*) and **Patrick Swayze.** Their animosity toward each other started in an earlier project they had done together. This time, it was so bad it almost ruined this movie. But, hey, they're actors and were finally able to fake a romance.

Later, Swayze ungallantly blamed it on Grey. In his autobiography, he said she was very emotional, sometimes bursting into tears if someone criticized her. At other times, he said she would start acting silly, laughing so much they'd have to do the scenes again. Hey, she sounds just like the young girl in love that she was playing!

Her moodiness may also have been a reaction to the difficult filming conditions. It was so hot on the set that one day ten people passed out in a half hour. Swayze himself had to go a hospital when he fell doing his own stunts.

Two other things about this movie:

The filming of the summer-fun movie ran into October, so they had to spray-paint the yellow leaves green so it wouldn't look like an Autumn Romance movie.

Most important, the "Jewish Catskills" movie that you're supposed to think was filmed at a place like Grossinger's, was shot in *goyishe* Virginia and North Carolina.

THE NOSE JOB FROM HELL You know the old expression: it's not who you know, it's who you know had a nose job? Well, no one knew **Jennifer Grey** after her nose job. Probably no star changed as much from a nose job as she did (except for **Tom Cruise, John Travolta,** and **Marilyn Monroe**). Grey's rhinoplasty was technically a good job, but after the surgery, she became so unrecognizable—and typical looking—that she's never had a major success since.

Contactmusic.com quoted her as saying: "I went in the operating theater a celebrity—and come out anonymous. It was like being in a witness protection program or being invisible. I'll always be this once-famous actress nobody recognizes...because of a nose job."

CASABLANCA WAS MORE JEWISH THAN YOU REALIZE Jews will always have *Casablanca* because so many of those involved in its production and acting were Jewish. Even a Jew came up with the idea for it. Before World War II started, a 27-year-old New York English teacher named **Murray Bennett** wrote an anti-Nazi play called *Everybody Comes to Rick's*. But he couldn't find a producer for the show. So he sold the script and story to Warner Brothers for $20,000 and they changed the name to *Casablanca*.

As for the actors, **Peter Lorre**, the weirdo petty thief with the letters of transit, was born a Jew named **László Löwenstein**.

The croupier Emil, who was shocked, *shocked* that gambling was going on, was not only played by a Jew, **Marcel Dalio,** born **Israel Moshe Blauschild,** but Dalio had to flee from France when the Germans put his picture up all over Paris with the words: "This is what a Jew looks like!"

Dalio was married to the Jewish woman who plays Yvonne, Rick's early lover in the movie, and in real life, the couple both had to leave France to escape the Nazis.

Conrad Veidt, who portrayed Major Strasser, was married to a Jew and they also had to get out of Germany before his wife and he were arrested...Many think the young Bulgarian couple, the Brandels—the woman who was supposed to "give herself up" to Captain Renault—was supposed to be Jewish. She was played by **Joy Page,** whose mother was Jewish...The character of Carl, Rick's trusted headwaiter, was played by **S.Z. Sakall**, a Hungarian Jew. **Curt Bois,** the pickpocket, was a German Jew.

Almost all those responsible for making the movie were also

Jewish. There was *Casablanca*'s executive producer, **Jack L. Warner,** and the producer, **Hal Wallis,** whose family changed their name from Walinsky. The studio could have ended up as "Walinsky Brothers" instead of "Warner Brothers"—and Time Warner could have been Time Walinsky.

The director, **Michael Curtiz,** was a Hungarian Jew whose sister's husband, her daughter, and two of her sons were killed in Auschwitz. The screenwriters were **Philip** and **Julius Epstein,** twins, and **Howard Koch.** The composer was **Max Steiner,** although "As Time Goes By," actually written seven years before this movie, was composed by someone who was probably a German Jew, **Herman Hupfeld**.

So, as time goes by, we realize more and more how much this 75-year-old movie was Jewish and speaks of those escaping persecution even today. Which makes it even more Jewish.

⚹ ⚹ ⚹

CLOSE CALLS...
THESE MOVIES WERE ALMOST TITLED...

The co-writer of *Annie Hall* offered some title suggestions that were far more Jewish than the eponymous one: *It Had to Be Jew* and *Me and My Goy*.

The movie *The Hangover* was retitled for Israel as *Before the Wedding We Stop in Vegas*.

West Side Story, the movie, and show, was originally intended to be Jews vs. Catholics rather than Americans vs. Puerto Ricans. The suggested title, *East Side Story*.

NON-JEWS IN HOLLYWOOD

ROBIN WILLIAMS ON HOLOCAUST MOVIES When the late **Robin Williams** was in *Jakob the Liar,* a movie based on a novel by a Holocaust survivor, he was interviewed by *Jewish Journal* on people's attitudes toward Holocaust movies.

"People say they've seen this before. But how many police movies do we see every year? How many exploding asteroids? People can tolerate that, but they say 'Oh God, another Holocaust film. Can't have that! Seen that!'"

SOME SHIKSA WIVES IN HOLLYWOOD When **Pamela Anderson** married **Rick Salomon,** for the second time, they took an El Al flight straight to Israel for their honeymoon. They stayed at the King David Hotel in Jerusalem to shoot an ad campaign and act as a judge on the Israeli version of *Dancing with the Stars*. But none of that makes her Jewish, which she's not, although she's been a good friend of Israel, helping to raise funds for the Israel Defense Forces.

But the groom, Rich Salomon, ah, *he's* Jewish, even though he was once married for four months to the shiksa of shiksas, **Paris Hilton**.

Drew Barrymore is married to **Will Kopelman,** whose father, **Arie Kopelman,** was the former head of Chanel. "I try to be a good shiksa wife," Barrymore told **Anne Cohen** of the *forward.com*.

Indeed, she goes to temple and even tried to make a Passover Seder when she and her husband were dating. "It was a disaster. And I [even] got the date wrong," she admitted.

It's amazing that **Steven Spielberg** would even marry again after suffering through one of the most costly Hollywood divorces ever. But he fell in love with the non-Jewish actress, **Kate Capshaw,** when he was directing *Indiana Jones*, and she converted. Together, they have seven children.

Another shiksa-wife isn't from Hollywood, but her father owns the equivalent of California's Hearst Castle in Palm Beach, the ornate Mar-a-Lago Club. An orthodox Rabbi converted **Ivanka Trump** in preparation for her marriage to *New York Observer* publisher **Jared Kushner**. Hopefully, her father, The Donald, was all fired up about his Jewish son-in-law. As for her, she said: "I'm a New Yorker, I'm in real estate. I'm as close to Jewish...as anyone can start off."

Here are a few more shiksa brides brought to you by

mybigfatjewishwedding.com.

Adam Sandler and **Jackie Titone's** wedding party included their bulldog wearing a yarmulke, and acting as ring bearer as he schlepped down the aisle with the ring.

Sacha Baron Cohen, or **Borat** and before that, **Ali G**, married **Isla Fisher**, who despite her name was not Jewish but she converted.

Seth Rogen & **Lauren Miller** married in a wedding officiated by a female Rabbi.

Natalie Portman and **Benjamin Millipied** were wrapped in a tallis during the service.

DO SHIKSAS GET MORE ROLES IN MOVIES? In *Seinfeld,* they called it "shiksappeal." But why Jewish women don't do better in Hollywood was discussed by actress **Rachel Weisz** in an interview excerpted here from *The Jewish Journal:*

WEISZ "In some way, acting is prostitution, and Hollywood Jews don't want their own women to participate. Also, there's an element of *Portnoy's Complaint*—they all fancy Aryan blondes."

ANTI-SEMITES IN MOVIES

JUST HOW ANTI-SEMITIC IS MEL GIBSON? In September 2009, Associated Press announced that actor **Mel Gibson** would be developing—directing and presumably acting in—a film about the life of Judah Maccabee, the victorious warrior celebrated at Hanukkah.

What a surprise that was! Remember that Gibson directed and personally funded a virulently anti-Semitic movie, *The Passion of the Christ,* which made $612 million dollars, so what did he care? Gibson was also caught on tape spewing anti-Semitic filth, not to mention his upbringing by a Holocaust-denying father whose views he appears to espouse.

Nothing further was heard about the movie until its well-known Jewish screenwriter, **Joe Eszterhas** (*Flashdance, Basic Instinct,* etc.,) announced in a 9-page public letter in *thewrap.com* that *The Maccabees* would never be made because "Gibson hates Jews." He said Gibson never intended to make the movie. "He was just trying to deflect continuing charges of anti-Semitism."

Brent Lang, who contributed to that story, said that Gibson "continually called Jews 'Hebes' and 'oven-dodgers' and 'Jewboys'...when we discussed someone, [he] asked, 'He's a Hebe, isn't he?'" Lang also said Gibson, too, was a Holocaust denier. And the final bombshell: before the movie was shelved, Eszterhas said Gibson told him he wanted to make *The Maccabees* because "What I really want to do with this movie is to convert the Jews to Christianity," he wrote in his sizzling Kindle single on Gibson: *Heaven and Mel.*

💻 THE WORST MEL GIBSON RANTS

...Bizarrely done to kittens (huh?)
http://tinyurl.com/37rgmrs

GENERAL GEORGE PATTON: YOU LOVED THE MOVIE, BUT YOU WOULD HAVE HATED THE GUY The movie *Patton* never reveals that the popular hero of World War II was seriously anti-Semitic. But **Richard Cohen,** in *The Washington Post,* quotes **General George Patton** in his letters to his wife as referring to the Jews in displaced person camps—some of whom had (barely) survived Auschwitz—as "like locusts," and "animals."

In fact, he saw Jews as even worse than animals. Referring to the lawyer appointed by **President Truman** to inspect the DP Displaced Persons (DP) camps, Patton wrote that "his ilk believe that the displaced person is a human being, which he is not, and this applies particularly to Jews who are lower than animals."

Aren't you sorry now that you loved the movie?

THE LUNATIC CRINGE

GWYNETH PALTROW BELIEVES YOU SHOULD TALK NICE TO WATER. *DUH....* According to *The Week,* American actress **Gwyneth Paltrow** believes in the, ahem, "science" promulgated by a controversial doctor named **Masaru Emoto.** Emoto says that using unkind phrases like "I hate you," and playing aggressive music, can damage water's molecular structure and make it behave differently. Sure.

Paltrow, who earlier also followed the insurance-agent-turned-Rabbi, **Philip Berg,** and his LA Kabbalah Center, once admitted on her website that she was "fascinated by [Emoto's] growing science..." *Science?* The *TheGuardian.com/UK* referred to him as a "quack-in-chief."

THE DAY WILLIAM SHATNER WAS "SAVED" BY A UFO
It's odd that two of the major *Star Trek* figures, **William Shatner** & **Leonard Nimoy,** who rocketed to outer space were both Jewish. Stranger still that one of them may have really been there. In outer space. As in la la land.

In 1969, William Shatner, aka James T. Kirk, not only told the TV show *One Step Beyond* that he saw a UFO, but also that he was telepathically saved by it. He was on a motorcycle trip in the Mojave Desert when his bike wouldn't start, he ran out of water and collapsed. Along came the United Federation of Planets starship *USS Enterprise*...well, not exactly. But he said on the show that a "shiny sleek craft" passed over him, telepathically directing him in a certain direction where there was a gas station, and he was saved.

JUST SO YOU SHOULD KNOW

WEIRD HEADLINE DEPARTMENT "Harvey Weinstein was thanked five times more than God" at 2013 Oscars.

Melanie Griffith, who's not Jewish but played a Jewish secretary turned Allied spy in *Shining Through*, said of the Holocaust: "I didn't know that 6 million Jews were killed." Her widely reported idiotic comment earned her the nickname "Brainiac" on the Internet.

According to *Stars of David*, **Leonard Nimoy's** Vulcan salute in *Star Wars* was introduced by Nimoy, who remembered seeing the Rabbis do it when they said the priestly blessings.

Dustin Hoffman got involved in acting because he took it as a "gut course" in college for the credits. He was told it was like gym—nobody fails you.

Daniel Day-Lewis, whose mother was Jewish, is known to always get completely into the role he's rehearsing. So when he was filming *My Left Foot,* about someone who could hardly move, Lewis wouldn't leave his wheelchair, so he had to be lifted around the set, and he also insisted on being spoon-fed.

Bernard Schwartz and **Rosetta Jacobs** instead of **Tony Curtis** and **Piper Laurie,** their real names, were jokingly listed on the marquee for *The Prince Who Was a Thief.* That was done at a movie theater on the Lower East Side, because that's where the two stars came from—and they were originally known by those names.

CHAPTER 3
THAT'S ENTERTAINMENT—MORE CELEBS

COMEDIANS

JERRY SEINFELD & FRIENDS, YADDA YADDA

WHEN JERRY SEINFELD WORKED ON A KIBBUTZ And he wasn't a very good kibbutznik. In 1970, when comedian **Jerry Seinfeld** was 16, he went to Israel and worked on a kibbutz, where he was remembered later as a "nudnik." He was..."like a cactus—not impressive, and no one paid attention to him," wrote **Jerry Oppenheimer** in his biography, *Seinfeld: The Making of a Comedian.* One woman there claimed Jerry was constantly making jokes that no one understood–and that only Jerry laughed at.

Jspacenews.com said he wasn't very good at his assignments, which was mostly to work on the banana groves at Kibbutz Sa'ar in Galilee. But Seinfeld explained that "Nice Jewish boys from Long Island don't like to get up at six in the morning to pick bananas. All summer long I found ways to get out of work."

Can you blame him? Naah..., as Jerry would have said. But according to Oppenheimer, Jerry *did* gain something from that summer. He may have lost his virginity "to a neurotic Jewish girl from Long Island." Sounds like one of his Seinfeld episodes.

THE "SEINFELD" GANG: JERRY, GEORGE, KRAMER, & ELAINE

Jerry Seinfeld recently made the list of the richest actors in the world, with an estimated wealth of 820 million dollars. The list, compiled by Wealth-X, also included another Jewish comedian, **Adam Sandler**, at #10, with $340 million.

Jerry turned down $5 million per episode to do another year or 22 episodes of Seinfeld. He obviously decided that a year of his life to do what he wanted was worth more than $100 million plus. Or maybe he simply decided that he had enough money (see item above). By the time the show ended, it was calculated that he made $13,000 for every line he delivered.

Julia Louis-Dreyfus, now the star of the hit show *Veep,* before that was best-known as Elaine on *Seinfeld,* may be worth about $200 million dollars. Her father is **Gerard Louis-Dreyfus,** Chairman of the Louis-Dreyfus Group, worth 4 billion dollars, a man who's obviously a master of his (financial) domain.

When **Larry David w**as a struggling writer, he was a bra salesman.

Jason Alexander, actually **Jay Scott Greenspan**, who played the hapless George Costanza, is a champion poker player. After *Seinfeld* ended, the rotund actor had more time to play in poker tournaments—and once snagged a $500,000 prize for his charity.

Michael Richards, best known as (Cosmo) Kramer, the rubbery-limbed, slovenly-looking neighbor—he always wore clothes one size too large to make him seem that way—stumbled into Jerry's apartment 380 times during the program's 180 episodes.

He always looked like he was about to fall, but he metaphorically did fall on his face when he gave a bizarre racist rant during a stand-up performance at a comedy club. It was secretly recorded by someone in the audience and widely reported afterward in the press. That, along with being identified so much with *Seinfeld,* pretty much ended his career, in which he was so identified as Kramer that someone once recognized him in the jungles of Bali.

Alas, most people think he's Jewish, partially because they think *Seinfeld* was "a Jewish show." He has also claimed to be Jewish–which he's not, thank you–and says he has adopted Judaism. But apparently, and happily, he hasn't done anything about it.

WERE THE CHARACTERS IN SEINFELD PSYCHOLOGICALLY DISTURBED? Was the *Seinfeld* gang highly neurotic? You betcha, believes one college professor, who teaches a course on "Psy-feld," analyzing Jerry's obsessive compulsive traits, Kramer's schizoid personality, Elaine's inability to forge meaningful relationships, and George's eccentricity.

NJ.com, said that **Dr. Anthony Tobias**, who teaches his students at Rutgers Robert Wood Johnson Medical School about psychiatric disorders through *Seinfeld*, describes the gang as "maladaptive at the individual level." The class doesn't only analyze the main characters, but also people like Newman ("very sick"), and Elaine's five boyfriends, whom he says are suffering from "delusional disorder."

WHO PLAYED SEINFELD'S "STEINBRENNER"? George Steinbrenner, the Yankee President who "appeared" faceless seven times on *Seinfeld* as a voice-over, always filmed from "his" back, was **Larry David**, the writer of *Seinfeld* and *Curb Your Enthusiasm*. But the "back and hands" guy was an actor who never received residuals for his role, and later tried to parlay his "fame" into some frontal roles. He never succeeded and instead drove motorhomes around the country for delivery.

✡ ✡ ✡

JON STEWART

HE WAS THE TOP JEW ON TV—HERE'S WHAT YOU DON'T KNOW ABOUT JON STEWART When **Jon Stewart** was in college, someone once called him a kike and commented on the size of his nose. Others around him nervously waited to see what he would say. He defused the situation by joking that "size" had never been an issue for him.

Stewart was widely expected to take over from the **David Letterman** show in 1993. But when the 6'4" **Conan O'Brien** got the job instead, the 5' 7" Stewart quipped: "I'm too short to host a late-night talk show. It's like the bar at an amusement-park ride. You have to be six foot two or over."

If you think Jon Stewart is smart, his father was an engineer who held 20 patents. From 2001 through 2008, **Donald Leibowitz** was a professor of physics at The College of New Jersey, before teaching an online course at Thomas Edison State College.

Stewart commissioned the man who edits the crossword puzzles for *The New York Times,* **Will Shortz,** to write a puzzle with a proposal in it for his girlfriend. **Tracey Mcshane**. She was a veterinary technician who once worked at the Bronx Zoo, and wasn't Jewish. But they both legally changed their names to Stewart. Stewart's name was actually originally spelled **Jonathan Stuart Leibowitz.**

Stewart had a checkered work career before he got into show biz. One of his earlier jobs had some bite: he was also a live mosquito sorter for the New Jersey Department of Health. Ouch.

At another time in his life, according to *jonstewart.net*, he was fired from six stores—in one mall! You can't blame them when as a shelf stocker at Woolworth's, he dove into a beanbag chair that hit an aquarium, causing $10,000 in damage. Not to mention all those dead fish on the floor. Who fired him? The assistant manager—his brother, **Larry.**

Anthony Weiner, the disgraced politician who never grew out of the childhood game of "show and tell" when he showed more than just his face in a selfie while the media gleefully did the "tell" was a close friend and college roommate of Stewart's.

SHOWS

POPULAR JEWS ON TV

EVERYBODY LOVED BRAD GARRETT IN EVERYBODY LOVES RAYMOND Yes, this 6' 8 ¼" Jewish actor, whose real name is **Bradley Harold Gerstenfeld,** shot up to fame as the policeman brother of Raymond in *Everybody Loves Raymond.* One of Garrett's most hilarious gigs was a 2-minute episode in *Seinfeld* as Jerry's car mechanic named Tony. Check "The Bottle Deposit" on YouTube.

🖥 http://tinyurl.com/pgvj2q7

MAD MEN'S MICHAEL GINSBURG HAS HIS OWN WINE LABEL If you were mad about *Mad Men*, then you know there was a Jewish copywriter on it named Michael Ginsberg. He was played by **Ben Feldman**, with a Brooklyn accent so thick you could cut it with a knife and spread it on a bagel. But in real life, he's more interested in wine than bagels.

Not satisfied to just drink it, Ben, and his lifelong friend set up a small winery, **Angelica Cellars**. And today it's sold "in a couple of cool restaurants," he says, and also online at *www.angelicacellars.com*.

In a video on *aol.com*, Feldman seems to suggest it was a choice between becoming a drunk or opening a wine cellar. And the latter was, well, more fruitful. "There comes a point when you're drinking so much that you have to stop and go, 'Is this gonna be a problem? Or do we need to make this into a sellable art?' And we chose the latter."

And it gave him something to whine about besides his ad agency job at *Mad Men*.

POPULAR TV SHOWS

THE REAL *DOWNTON ABBEY* CASTLE WAS PROBABLY SAVED BY THE ILLEGITIMATE DAUGHTER OF A FAMOUS JEW *Downton Abbey*, the incredibly popular BBC show that also aired on PBS in the US is based on Highclere Castle, where they shot most of the indoor scenes in the show.

Highclere's most famous earlier inhabitant was **George Herbert**, the Fifth Earl of Carnarvon. He was an Egyptologist, best known as the financial backer for the excavation of the tomb of **Tutankhamun or King Tut**. But on the Internet, which delights in bizarre trivia, he's almost as famous for accidentally cutting himself shaving, which infected his mosquito bite, leading to his death at the age of 56 from blood poisoning.

Digging up tombs costs money, and so does keeping up 5,000 acres with a 12,000 square foot castle with over 50 bedrooms and 25 bathrooms. The *Forward.com* revealed that Herbert wisely chose to marry a wealthy woman so he wouldn't have to hock his blue china and could keep that castle up and stocked in Beluga caviar and Château Lafite Rothschild.

This wife, **Almina Victoria Maria Alexandra Wombwell's** hand came with a £500,000 dowry, no paltry sum at the time. It was easy for her to acquire because her real father was the famed fabulously wealthy Jewish banker, **Alfred de Rothschild**.

That enabled the Earl of Carnarvon to maintain the castle and go about digging up cursed mummies. She became the high society hostess who held all those fancy dinner parties on which those in *Downton Abbey* are loosely based.

NOTE: TV imitates life. In the fake *Downton Abbey*, the father of Lady Cora (Lord Grantham's wife) was "Isidore Levinson, a dry goods multimillionaire from Cincinnati." The Dowager Countess (**Dame Maggie Smith**) must have practically plotzed when her son married a Jew, but he needed "the heiress Cora to avail himself of her fortune, needed to pay the upkeep on the castle he inherited," said the *Forward.com*.

LISA KUDROW OF *FRIENDS* HAD A "DRIVE BY" BAR MITZVAH Usually when you hear someone was in a drive-by, you think chalk outlines on the sidewalk, police and drug deals gone wrong. So you wonder when you hear **Lisa Kudrow,** aka Phoebe from *Friends* say her son was in a drive-by. It turns out to be "drive-by bar mitzvah."

Her son was wandering around a mall when Chabad, an Orthodox, Hasidic organization, asked him if he was Jewish. (Do they have some criteria for this? Are they using *Jewdar?*) When he confirmed that he was on his mother's side, they offered to do a bar mitzvah right there, complete with laying tefillin (those little boxes with Torah verses in them) and wearing a *kippah* (yarmulke).

Any Gentiles reading this don't have to worry that it isn't safe to go to the mall now without coming home Hasidic. They do ask permission first, you need the bona fides, and oh, yes, you have to agree.

"FOREIGN" TV SHOWS

***HEIL HITLER*, THE NAZI-THEMED TV SHOW YOU NEVER SAW...Fortunately.** As the show and film *The Producers* proved with their iconic song "Springtime for Hitler," even Nazi Germany can be made to be funny—in the right (Jewish) hands. However, **Mel Brooks** is probably the only one who could have pulled this off. A British sitcom involving **Hitler** and **Eva Braun,** entitled *Heil Honey I'm Home!* did not.

It only played for a grand total of one episode in 1990. The series provoked immediate outrage, and the BBC promptly canceled it.

Did anyone think that there was anyone out there who would think it funny to transplant loveable Adolf and Eva to a suburban setting, like that of *The Honeymooners,* and dub in canned laughter?

The premise was that this "hilarious" Hitler isn't very good at getting along with his neighbors, Arny, and Rosa Goldstein. Imagine that! Then watch the sidesplitting antics as Hitler, known for being a teensy weensy bit un-fond of Jews, tries to borrow a cup of sugar, or whatever Hitler does in a nice suburb. The never-aired episodes included a plot by Hitler to kill the Goldsteins, because some idiot thought what could be funnier than that? *Surprise*: hilarity failed to ensue.

***HOMELAND* AND *IN TREATMENT* BOTH STARTED IN ISRAEL** "Homeland," a complex psychological drama about a soldier who returns after eight years of being held captive by terrorists is actually based on *Hatufim* (Prisoners of War), about three Israeli soldiers captured when a secret mission in Lebanon went awry. As *Haaretz.com* says: "The Israeli version "...is far more interested in the psyche of a country than a potential psycho returning from captivity."

"In Treatment" was originally an Israeli television series about a psychologist who is in serious need of mental help himself. (Know any?) The original, called *BeTipul* in Hebrew, was picked up by HBO in 2008.

JUST SO YOU SHOULD KNOW

If not for Jews, we wouldn't have had **The Maury Povich** TV show. Not just because he's Jewish, but because in 1930, a Jew, **Karl Landsteiner,** discovered human blood groups. Without those, it would have been impossible to establish whose child someone is—so there would have gone Maury's show!

The network originally wanted *The Nanny* to be about an Italian instead of a Jew, or as one reviewer put it, pizza pie versus knishes.

Soupy Sales (**Milton Supman**) sons' nicknames were **Hambone, Chicken Bone,** and **Soup Bones.**

Rob Morrow, a nice Jewish boy from New Rochelle, who's best known for playing a nice Jewish doctor in Alaska in *Northern Exposure,* named his daughter **Tu,** as in Tu-morrow. His wife's name is **Debbon Ayer,** as in Debonair.

Jerry Springer of the TV slug-fest show where people knock each other down, once got (metaphorically) knocked down himself. While he was a Councilman in Cincinnati, he foolishly wrote a personal check to a prostitute, and the check turned up during a raid. He resigned, but his honesty about it helped him win the election. In 1979, he was actually the Mayor of Cincinnati.

FIDDLING AROUND

FASCINATING FACTS ABOUT *FIDDLER ON THE ROOF*...after 50 years, it's nice to know. *Fiddler*...recently celebrated its 50th anniversary since its Broadway debut. **Cindy Adams,** writing in "Page Six" in the *New York Post,* had some interesting things to say about the iconic Jewish musical.

Theodore Bikel, who played the hapless milkman Tevye 2,000 times—more than any other actor—told Adams he understood shtetl life because his model was his religious grandfather, who gave up going to the synagogue for two years. "God has given up on our people, so I abandon God," his grandfather said. Then his grandfather returned to his faith. "You can't get more Tevye than that," she wrote.

From 1966 to 1969, **Bette Midler** played the role of the daughter Tzeitel in *Fiddler*...When her sister came to New York to see her perform, her sister was killed by a taxi.

Luther Adler, who played Tevye in the first national company, tried to put his own stamp on the production by making the outrageous suggestion that the most popular song, "If I Were a Rich Man" should go. Instead, *he* was the one to go after only a few weeks.

Richard Dreyfuss, Rob Reiner, and **John Ritter** all auditioned for the movie role of Motel the Tailor. Instead, the part went to the lesser-known **Leonard Frey.**

One proposed early name for *Fiddler on the Roof* was *Where Poppa Came From.*

SUCH A *SHONDA* Jerome Robbins may have done a wonderful job as the choreographer for *Fiddler*...(along with *West Side Story, King & I, Gypsy,* etc.), but as a person, feh. This self-denying Jew was so terrified of being outed as gay that when he was called before Congress investigating communists (the "Blacklist"), he named more names than any other witnesses.

And how many people did **Zero Mostel**, (*Fiddler on the Roof, How to Succeed in Business, The Producers*) name? None. Now, *there's* a mensch.

IS *DOWNTON ABBEY* A WASP *FIDDLER ON THE ROOF?*
Whether the popular BBC series *Downton Abbey* is a goyishe version of *Fiddler* was a questin asked by **Michael L. Millenson,** who pointed out that both were about proud men with three daughters in changing times.

Writing in the *Forward.com,* Millenson points out that the fate of the three daughters in two fictional stories, both taking place before World War I,)is remarkably similar. Both Tzeitel and Lady Mary are urged to marry someone they don't love--the butcher Lazar Wolf and the newspaper magnate, Sir Richard Carlisle--but refuse. Two other daughters (Hodel and Lady Sybil) fall in love with—and marry—radicals, Perchik who opposes the Czar, and Branson who wants to free Ireland. And both Chava and Lady Edith ultimately choose "inappropriate" partners, a non-Jew and a married man.

Why don't Tevye and Lord Grantham initially want to go along with the choices that make their daughters happy? Because in all cases, their choices go against..."Tradition...."

MUSIC
FAMOUS SINGERS & SONGS

BARBRA STREISAND'S COUSIN WAS REFUSED ISRAELI CITIZENSHIP Why? It's hard to imagine a celebrity more Jewish than **Barbra Streisand**, since it's as obvious as the nose on her face. (Sorry). But what about her cousin, **Dale Streisand**? His Jewish name is **Da'el Yochai** and nothing is more Jewish than that.

Since Jews can invoke the "right of return" to claim Israeli citizenship, a Streisand cousin moving to Israel should be a no brainer. Apparently not, since the Israeli authorities denied his request to immigrate (aliyah) with his Filipino wife and daughter. Barbra is worth about $340 million and one of the most famous people in the world. Can't she pull a couple of strings for her hippie cousin?

Maybe not, after Israeli authorities found a reference to a Christian missionary organization on his Facebook page, which has since wisely been deleted. And then, there's also his past in the Hare Krishnas. But Dale now claims to be Orthodox, and that the references to the organizations were inadvertent. He just clicked something a friend sent him titled "Click if you love **Jesus**." Yeah, everyone does that.

The authorities said: "An individual's relationship with Christians does not revoke his right to immigrate." But the Interior Ministry still denied his application in February 2011. After more legal wrangling and appearing in person in Israel's Supreme Court, he got the right to enter Israel and make his application from inside the country as of January 2014. But even then, instead of getting the general visa he was supposed to, he entered on a tourist visa. He says he wants to be a tour guide when he gets his citizenship. The perfect job for people who like people.

DID A LION PROVE A FAMOUS "JEWISH" SINGER WAS LYING? Do you think when things get really hairy, some Jewish converts secretly return to their roots? That's what may have happened with a famous convert, **Sammy Davis Jr**.

According to *Hollywood Stories,* Davis, a famous black one-eyed song-and-dance man who converted to Judaism after almost dying in a car accident, posed with the MGM lion for a promotional piece. When the lion suddenly growled (as he should have) and got into a pouncing position (as he shouldn't have), Sammy became a fraidy cat where the lion was concerned. Fearful he would become lion meat, this new Jew quickly crossed himself.

Supposedly, when Davis told the story to his friend, **Frank Sinatra,** Sinatra asked him why, as a Jew, he had made the sign of the cross. Davis said: "I didn't have time to make a Star of David."

WHY WAS A MELON NAMED AFTER JUSTIN TIMBERLAKE?) *The Jerusalem Post (jpost.com)* announced that some Israeli farmers had named a melon after **Justin Timberlake**. "It's yellow on the outside, orange on the inside, and has a three-week shelf life." *Heeb,* a satirical magazine, wrote: "It's worth pointing out that Justin himself has slightly different coloration, and...has enjoyed a shelf life of twenty years and counting."

Recently, a praying mantis was named after Jewish supreme court judge, **Ruth Bader Ginsburg.** So when will they name something after **Mick Jagger,** who was so popular in Israel? Wrote **ZayinB'Ain**:"I'm not sure they even make prunes in Israel, anyways."

FUNNY
JEWISH SONGS
YOU PROBABLY NEVER HEARD

Here are a few novelty songs written by people with names like The Beach Boychicks, Guns & Charoses, and Shlock Rocka. The songs have titles like the following:

They Ain't Making Jews Like Jesus Anymore
Shleppin' My Baby Back Home
Duvid Crockett
Be True to Your Shul
Pretty Fly for a Rabbi
Man of Constant Tsuris
It's Good to be a Jew at Christmas
How Much is That Pickle in the Window?
Shake your Tuchas; [sic]
Jap Rap; Ma is Playing Mahjong, an Eddie Cantor song.

JUST SO YOU SHOULD KNOW

Few would have been surprised if **Barbra Streisand** had ended up as a Rebbetzin, but as a First Lady? It almost happened.

In 1969, she began a relationship with then Canadian Prime Minister, **Pierre Trudeau.** He supposedly proposed. She may have considered it, too, because she began learning French. But she ultimately refused the proposal.

Teen heartthrob-singer-songwriter **Justin Bieber** claims that he says the *Shema* each day. Long story not worth going into.

Eice Charry and **Noah Kaminsky** are not names you know, but that's because the singer decided to discard those and sing under his real name, **Neil Diamond.**

CHAPTER 4
ROYALTY & POLITICIANS

ACROSS THE POND

WAS LITTLE PRINCE GEORGE, KATE AND WILLIAM'S SON CIRCUMCISED? Like his grandfather, Prince Charles Why would there even be a question of circumcising a British royal since they're obviously not Jewish, and circumcision isn't that popular across the pond. But as a status symbol, the British royal family has traditionally circumcised their children.

Surprisingly, though, **Prince Charles** and his brothers, **Prince Andrew,** and **Prince Edward** *were* all circumcised. Indeed, it was widely reported that a mohel from London's Jewish community was chosen over the royal physician to do the snipping, probably leaving the royal physician a bit snippy himself.

So, the big question is, was the new prince also cut? He probably would have been, had not the tradition of royal circumcision been stopped by **Diana,** Princess of Wales, who didn't allow her sons, **Prince William** or **Prince Harry** to undergo this *rite de passage.* So, if Harry and Willy didn't have their willies shortened when they were born, the answer is probably no. According to the *jewishpress.com,* Little **Prince George** is probably intact since his grandparents had cut off the cut-off.

Yet you can be sure that if little Prince George was indeed secretly circumcised, while it may have once again been done by a rabbi, there was definitely no bris.

IS PRINCE WILLIAM'S WIFE, PRINCESS KATE (MIDDLETON) REALLY JEWISH? That's what people say. Around the time of The Wedding, there were a lot of reports (and hand-wringing) in Great Britain over the possibility that **Prince William's** wife, **Kate Middleton,** the Duchess of Cambridge, was Jewish. Or at least partially so. It was pointed out in the press that Kate's mother's maiden name before it was Middleton was "**Goldsmith.**"

Indeed, the totally unreliable *Iranian Mehr News Agency* went so far as to declare that not only was Kate a Sephardic Jew from her mother's side, but that the timing of the wedding was based on "Jewish culture." Oh, come on...

Then, feeding fuel to the anti-Semitic fire, came a widely quoted statement by a BBC royal correspondent, **Michael Cole**. He declared that Kate's mother, **Carole Middleton,** was the daughter of **Ronald Goldsmith** and **Dorothy Harrison**, both Jews, and that *their* parents were Jewish. Plus, that her mother was descended from the **Myers**, who were a distinguished nineteenth-century Jewish family.

But no real expert agrees that she's Jewish on the matriarchal side. Even Cole, when interviewed by **Miriam Shaviv** for The *TimesofIsrael.com,* admitted the evidence was circumstantial.

Harder evidence came from the former Chairman of the Jewish Genealogical Society of Great Britain, **Laurence Harris**. "There is no evidence of Jewish branches in Kate's family tree," he declared. Pointing out that Jewish surnames were also used by non-Jews, he said there was no record of synagogue marriages or Jewish burials in her family.

So much for all the Internet forums on whether Queen-to-be Kate was "tainted by Jewish blood." The *TimesofIsrael.com* probably best summed the issue up when they said, "Middleton, Shmiddleton....Despite the claims of dubious experts, unnamed Sephardi rabbis, and an Iranian news agency, **Prince George** will not be England's very first Yiddishe monarch."

ELIZABETH, THE QUEEN OF ENGLAND, HAS VISITED 130 COUNTRIES—BUT NEVER ISRAEL. THINK IT'S AN OVERSIGHT? Think again. They don't call. They don't write. It would be nice if the Brits officially visited the country that rejected them. But while Her Majesty, **Queen Elizabeth II,** has visited over 130 countries in her 50 plus years on the throne, she has never once come to the Holy Land.

True, there were two royal visits from others—but they hardly count. Once was when **Prince Philip**, her-husband-who-must-always-walk-one-step-behind-her, came to Israel in 1993. That was because his mother was being honored as a Righteous Gentile for hiding three Jews in the palace in Athens during the Nazi occupation. **Schindler**, she wasn't, but three is still better than none.

Then there was the time that **Prince Charles** visited the Holy Land in 1995—but that was only to attend the funeral of Prime Minister **Yitzhak Rabin.** They were hardly doing Israel a symbolic favor, though, because they kept emphasizing that their visits were private and didn't represent the palace. Could the Brits have been worried that anything that would seem to legitimize Israel might hurt their doing business in the Arab world?

Still, one can hope that things might change one day. An optimistic entrepreneur once created an infant garment, emblazoned: "His Royal Highness. Future Birthright Israel Participant, 2031."

THE CLINTONS

WAS CHELSEA CLINTON'S INTERMARRIAGE GOOD FOR THE JEWS? When **Chelsea Clinton** became engaged to **Marc Mezvinsky**, the grandson of a Jewish Iowa grocer, *New York* magazine bemoaned the loss to intermarriage of one more Jew. **Jennifer Senior** wrote, "No matter: This is one of those instances where the prize—the First Daughter!—outshines the loss to the tribe, like when **Arthur Miller** wed **Marilyn Monroe**."

Their wedding ceremony included a *Ketubah* (Jewish marriage contract) and chuppah (wedding canopy). An editorial in the *forward.com* called the Clinton-Mezvinsky marriage "a milestone of sorts, a measure of social acceptance, a sign that we've arrived."

Not everyone was so happy about it. *The New York Times* pointed out: "Some Jews fear that the societal openness confirmed by high-profile intermarriages like that of Ms. Clinton and Mr. Mezvinsky, or **Caroline Kennedy** and **Edwin A. Schlossberg** in 1986, prod more Jews to marry out of their faith."

A Brooklyn-based orthodox newspaper was absolutely furious with Chelsea Clinton when she got pregnant later. "Chelsea Clinton Pregnant With Non-Jewish Child" they headlined, pointing out that that the interfaith marriage was "effectively pruning away that 3,300-year-old Jewish branch of the Mezvinsky family."

It could have been worse—and it was. One anti-Semitic website trumpeted the event as "Chelsea Clinton pregnant with Jew spawn."

THE BIZARRE CASE OF CHELSEA CLINTON'S FATHER-IN-LAW AND THE NIGERIAN E-MAIL SCAM There's no indication that the **Clinton** family had any qualms about their daughter **Chelsea** marrying a Jew, but they may have some concerns about the family she was marrying into. The groom's father, **Ed Mezvinsky,** a lawyer and a politician, fell for a bizarre Nigerian e-mail scam many years ago, losing 3 million dollars. But this story is even worse than that.

In this "black money" come-on, marks are told that money has been coated with black ink so it could be smuggled out of Nigeria, and then super-expensive chemicals to clean the ink off are sold to the sucker.

After he lost a bundle to that, and similar Nigerian scams, he himself became a conman, utilizing a Madoff-style Ponzi scheme to raise the money to pay himself back for his loss from these frauds. Almost as bad, he also used the Clinton name to get people to trust him and give him money.

Later, he claimed that part of the reason he acted like this was that he was diagnosed with bipolar disorder. But the judge wouldn't allow a mental illness defense. So in 2001, Mezvinsky's father pleaded guilty to 31 counts of fraud, involving almost $10 million, and was sentenced to five years in jail—which he did. He was also ordered to pay complete restitution to his victims—which he did not. He was released in 2008.

And yes, he not only went to his son **Marc's** wedding two years later, but along with the bride, Chelsea, and groom, **Marc,** and his new mishpocha, **Bill,** and **Hillary,** he danced the hora and went up in the chairs.

Which was probably a lot more fun for him than when he went up the river.

A SOPHISTICATED POLITICIAN LIKE BILL CLINTON SHOULD KNOW BETTER THAN TO MAKE A JEWISH "JOKE" LIKE THIS It's hard to believe a savvy politician like **Bill Clinton** would ever make a joke that could be construed as anti-Semitic—and to a Jewish audience no less! But a book called *Clinton Inc.* said he did exactly that.

Clinton told the joke in 2003 to a group of Jewish Republicans. A reporter from *The Weekly Standard* was present, who reported that Clinton told that awful (and old!) "joke" about the two Jews walking by a church that was offering $100 to people who converted.

Clinton should have stopped there—no, actually, he never should have started the joke—but he continued with the line about the Jew taking money after converting. His friend then asked for half, and the new convert then said to him, "You Jews...It's all about money." No one in the audience laughed.

✡ ✡ ✡

PRACTICALLY PRESIDENTS

DID THE ISRAELIS SPY ON AL GORE WHILE HE WAS IN THE BATHROOM? This story sounds too weird to be true—but those are the ones that often are true—of some Israeli guy crawling through an air duct spying on a guy on the john? And the guy on the john just happened to have been... **Al Gore.**

Newsweek quoted a "senior former U.S. intelligence operative" and whom can you trust if not an anonymous spook? He claimed another Secret Service agent on the toilet heard an odd sound from the air duct of Al Gore's bathroom, where the Secret Service agent was conducting some private business after the rest of his team had left. Looking up, the agent saw someone unclipping the vent. From the inside. Then a guy started coming out of the vent.

In the spirit that nothing is true until it has been officially denied, Retired Major General **Amos Yadlin**, former head of Israeli Military Intelligence, said that the tale was "delusional," "absolutely baseless," and strange. Which means it could be true. Yeah, sure, we all know that Israel does not spy on the United States at all.

At least, not since that **Jonathan Pollard** thing. And perhaps this is a good place to mention that famous headline reported by *israelnationalnews.com* on Pollard's spying on the US for Israel. "Iranian spy to serve 10 years; Pollard serving 29."

Now, what does a Secret Service agent do when he sees someone, who is probably another spy, coming out of a vent in a famous person's bathroom? Shoot a poison dart from a gun disguised as a pen? Report him? In real life—if this indeed happened in real life—the guy coming out of the vent coughed when he realized he was caught. Some kind of a signal? And then he crawled back into the vents.

A story like this could be embarrassing if it got out. Which it did. But as the anonymous source said, "You can't embarrass an Israeli. You catch them red-handed, and they shrug and say, 'Okay now, anything else?'"

True or not, you probably won't see this story reenacted in a Bond movie.

COMEDIAN-IN-CHIEF?

50,000 IDIOTS VOTED FOR ROSEANNE BARR FOR PRESIDENT OF AMERICA *(Bet you didn't even know that she ran.)* Most people were unaware of it, but comedian **Roseanne Barr** campaigned for President of the United States in the 2012 general election—and amazingly, placed sixth. Somehow, she got almost 50,000 votes, although she received zero percent of the popular vote. Still, almost 50,000 people were crazy enough or disillusioned enough to vote for the Domestic Goddess. Is there reason to be concerned about the possibility of her being President one day? Maybe anyone would be better than some of those who have made it so far.

DID POLITICAL WANNABE MICHELE BACHMAN'S "JEWISH" NAME KEEP MITT ROMNEY FROM BEING PRESIDENT? **Michele Bachmann**, a Lutheran, has been to Israel many times. In 1974, she spent the summer in a kibbutz, although it was under the sponsorship of a Christian ministry. But because of that, and mostly because her name could easily be Jewish, during the 2012 campaign there was supposed concern among Republicans that this Republican Minnesota congressman was siphoning off voters from **Mitt Romney's** campaign because Jews were supporting her instead of him in the mistaken belief that she was Jewish.

THEY'VE GOT CHOOT-SPA! HILARIOUS MISPRONUNCIATIONS

Bachmann, who has been after the Jewish vote (what politician in America isn't?) might have done better among Jews if she had pronounced Chutzpah correctly. No, it's not "Choot-spa" as she said.

How about the weird **Dr. Ben Carson** who wanted to be President of the United States? If he really wanted that Jewish endorsement when he was speaking before a Republican Jewish Coalition, he shouldn't have confused "Hamas," the terrorist group with "Hummus," the chickpea dish. Is there a Hummus terror threat we don't know about? And should Jews worry about what's happening in Baba Ghanoush and Tabouli?

Hillary Clinton didn't do so well either, even after supposedly taking Yiddish lessons to get closer to Jewish voters. Saying "kvell" with an extra syllable, as "ka-vell" probably lost those points she tried to gain.

Still, he made less of a fool of herself than Governor **Scott Walker,** when he wrote to a Jewish leader and instead of Mazel Tov signed it, "Thank you again and Malotov."

Joked (the non-Jewish) **Stephen Colbert** of this faux-pas: "He's still learning... he's a real munch, although he doesn't wear a yamaha... or observe the sherbert...[or]...Chanukah [where] you eat potato *chotchkes* and spill the dildo.... To my Jewish viewers...I say a hardy l'chaimlich maneuver...."

JEWISH HISTORY

JOSEPH STALIN'S JEWISH GRANDSON Joseph Stalin, leader of the Soviet Union for over 30 years, and possibly responsible for 20-60 million deaths, happily was not Jewish, although some say he was, but some say just about everyone was.

Regardless of his ancestry, this 5'4" club-footed tyrant with a withered arm had a daughter named **Svetlana.** She fell in love with a Jew. While some Christian fathers, especially tyrant ones, don't like their daughters dating Jews, this is a man who could and did do something about it: he had him arrested for alleged espionage and sent to Siberia for five to 10 years.

Undaunted, Svetlana married *another* Jew, a doctor, and they had one child together**, Josif,** before divorcing. He died in 2008 seemingly leaving no heirs, which would have been a relief to Stalin had he known.

COULD A LEV BRONSTEIN HAVE STARTED A REVOLUTION? He was such a nice Jewish boy, and his second marriage was even performed by a Jewish chaplain, but such a shonda. **Lev Bronstein** changed his name after he was 21. And with the new name of **Leon Trotsky,** it was probably easier for him to become a key leader of the Communist revolution in 1917 than if the name had stayed the same of that nice little Jewish boy he once was.

LISTEN MY CHILDREN AND YOU SHALL HEAR, OF THE MIDNIGHT RIDE OF...ISRAEL BISSELL?

Every schoolchild is taught about **Paul Revere's** famous ride in 1775, when he set out from Boston to Lexington to alert the countryside of the impending arrival of the British at Lexington and Concord. (Spoiler warning: the Americans won.)

But no one's ever heard of a man named **Israel Bissell**, a Jew, whose supposed ride at the same time for the same reason to announce the advent of the same enemy was longer in time and distance. But noooo, no one ever wrote a poem about him that would have made *him* famous. Except for a joking one by poet and historian **Clay Perry...**

> Listen, my children, to my epistle.
>
> Of the long, long ride of Israel Bissell,
>
> who out rode Paul by miles and time
>
> But didn't rate a poet's rhyme.

Here's the story. On April 19, 1775, Bissell claimed that he began a four-day horseback journey from Watertown, Massachusetts to Philadelphia along the Old Post Road to report the same battle that Revere was warning about.

True, some who have investigated this claim believe that it was an "Isaac" or "Trail" Bissell. But *some* Bissell seems to have been there, since history records messages from "Israel Bissell" all over the place. However, eyewitnesses don't, so maybe he remained safe at home in Connecticut and faked the ride.

He may have also faked his expense account. So what else is new? Bissell billed two pounds and one shilling for six days of expenses. But he couldn't have made it to Philly in the time he claimed. As it turns out, the Provincial Congress of Massachusetts wasn't any more honest, bouncing their check to him so he never got his money. Which would be poetic justice if he never made the ride.

But maybe he did. And why wasn't *some* Bissell honored? Did Revere become famous because his name sounded better, not to mention (but we must), less Jewish? As comedian **Robert Wuhl** noted, it might just be that Bissell's name "sounds too much like a Jewish vacuum cleaner."

JUST SO YOU SHOULD KNOW

The first cousin of the famous old-time movie star, **Lauren Bacall,** aka **Betty Perske,** was **Shimon Peres,** Prime Minister of Israel. The *forward.com* wrote that Peres came from her estranged father's side of the family, the Perskes. Although she avoided them most of her life, she later visited Peres socially in Israel.

Princess (and movie star) **Grace Kelly's** granddaughter is a half-Jewish royal. Monaco's **Charlotte Casiraghi** and (Jewish) comedian **Gad Elmaleh** have a son named **Raphael.** While it's true that his mother is only fifth in line to the throne, and the throne is about half the size of Central Park in New York, still, it's a (royal) start.

CHAPTER 5

JEW-BILATION—MORE MEMBERS OF THE TRIBE

✡

JEWS IN CHAI PLACES

WHO ARE THE TOP JEWS IN THE WORLD?

The *forward.com* in their always interesting "Shmooze" section, reported on the results of 11,000 people surveyed by an MIT Media Lab. They found that actress **Natalie Portman** ranked higher than former Prime Minister of Israel, **Ariel Sharon;** that **Moses** beat **Muhammad;** and that **Jesus Christ** won the top spot for Jews.

Michael Kaplan broke the list down further.

THE WORLD'S TOP FIVE JEWS

1) **Jesus Christ** 2) **Moses** 3) **Abraham** 4) **Albert Einstein** 5) **Karl Marx**

AMERICA'S TOP FIVE JEWS

1) **Stanley Kubrick** 2) **Isaac Asimov** 3) **Steven Spielberg** 4) **Noam Chomsky** 5) **Zac Efron**

ISRAEL'S TOP FIVE JEWS

1) **Solomon** 2) **Mary** 3) **John the Baptist** 4) **Mary Magdalene** 5) **Isaac**

THE TOP 10 JEWS ON *FORBES* BILLIONAIRES LIST *Forbes* magazine's annual list of billionaires includes several Jews. Here are the top ten from the 2015 list, singled out by *jta.org*. **Larry Ellison,** CEO of Oracle Corporation, **Michael Bloomberg,** American business magnate, politician (Former Mayor of New York City) and philanthropist), **Mark Zuckerberg:** Founder of Facebook, **Sheldon Adelson:** Chairman and CEO of the Las Vegas Sands Corporation, **Larry Page:** (mother Jewish) Co-founder of Google), **Sergey Brin:** Co-founder of Google, **George Soros:** Chairman of Soros Fund Management, **Carl Icahn:** Major shareholder of Icahn Enterprises, **Len Blavatnik:** Access Industries, **Michael Dell:** Computer corporation founder.

NAMES OF FAKE JEWISH SUPERHEROES Acidic Jew, Magen David, Matzah woman, Masada, Menorah man, Ragman, Sabraman, Shaloman, Superrabbi

---

Big D

Three Texans are boasting about their real estate. "My name is Roger," says the first. "I own 100,000 acres. They call my place 'The Jolly Roger.'

"The second Texan says: "My name is John. I own 200,000 acres, and they call my place 'Big John's.'

"The Jewish man says: "My name is Irving, and I own only 900 acres."

The other two look at him, disbelievingly. "Only 900 acres? What do you call your place?"

"Downtown Dallas," said the Jew.

QUESTIONS

WHAT WERE ALBERT EINSTEIN'S DYING WORDS? Comedian **Richard Lewis's** grandfather lived to 103 after eating a raw onion and smoking a cigar each day. What were his dying words? Lewis joked: "No one knows because no one would get near him."

That joke was almost true for **Albert Einstein,** except it was a language problem that prevented someone from hearing his dying words. No one knows what this Jewish genius's last words were since he spoke them in German. The nurse couldn't understand the language, so we'll never know what he said.

Maybe he changed his mind and decided it was $E = mc^3$?

THEY HAD MONEY PROBLEMS

WELL-KNOWN SUCCESSFUL JEWS WHO WENT BANKRUPT--and what happened to Oskar Schindler? The late humorist **Joey Adams** (his wife is *New York Post* columnist **Cindy Adams)**, once said that bankruptcy was a legal proceeding "whereby you put your money in your pants pocket and give your coat to your creditors." Here are a few who gave up their coats— and everything else—ending up with no pot to you-know-what in.

WE'D ALL BE BRITISH IF NOT FOR HAYMAN SALOMON: It is generally accepted that we might not have won the Revolutionary War if not for the financial contributions of a Polish immigrant named **Hayman Salomon**. He converted the French loans into immediate cash, thereby aiding the Continental Congress—and came up with the money to save this new country from collapse.

Unfortunately, partially because his huge below-market interest loans to the government were never repaid, he died bankrupt at the age of 45. His remains were deposited in some burial ground, and no one even knows where.

REMEMBER THE CITROEN CAR? Did you ever ride in that smooth vehicle that made you feel as if you were suspended? Alas, **André-Gustave Citroen**, a French Jew, was not as smooth as his eponymous car. Although he manufactured important munitions, popularized the automobile in Europe, pioneered mass production there, and the concept of after-sales service (warranties), he was addicted to gambling and led a lavish lifestyle. *Time* Magazine actually called him "the flashy little Jew." His company went bankrupt during the Great Depression and he lost control of it.

POOR DEER: THE AUTHOR PRACTICALLY GAVE "BAMBI" AWAY! Felix Salten, who wrote *Bambi,* realized that as a controversial Jew in Europe, they were going to come after him and his books. According to the *Jewish Review of Books,* Salten had to tie up his affairs quickly and move to a safer place in the '30s.

As he foresaw, his books were indeed banned, and he had to sell the film rights at a rock bottom price. The new owner transferred the rights to **Walt Disney**—who hated hunting and, therefore, loved the book. And Disney never gave Salten a dime for the movie.

HELLO MUDDAH, HELLO FADDAH! Allan Sherman became a sensation in the '50s with his song "Hello Muddah Hello Faddah," which was a huge hit on a record, which is what they called those large round things in those days. The album was titled *My Son the Folk Singer.* Sherman also conceived and produced the hit TV series *I've Got a Secret,* which was on the air for 15 years. Yet he died at 48 while living on unemployment insurance.

SOMEONE ACTUALLY DEVELOPED THOSE AWFUL THINGS: You probably haven't heard of **Marc Roth** although he has that kind of Jewish name that makes you think you know him. But if you've been to New York and taken a taxi cab, he's the one who developed those irritating touch screens in the back seat. Unfortunately, his $25 million dollar business failed, and he ended up homeless. He's now working to help other homeless people receive tech training.

HE WASN'T JEWISH, BUT OSKAR SCHINDLER MUST BE ON THIS LIST Thanks to the movie, no one will ever forget **Oskar Schindler** who saved 1200 Jews. They may have had 7,000 descendants, but he ended up with bubkes. His entire fortune—perhaps over 1 million dollars—was spent on bribes and black-market purchases, and he received only $15,000 back from a Jewish organization.

After the war, he emigrated to Argentina and tried raising chickens but went bankrupt. Then he got stuck with a cement factory that also went kaput. He ultimately lived on donations sent to him by his descendants.

THEY ALSO HAD TSURIS

COCKAMAMIE FEARS OF JEWS YOU (MOSTLY) THOUGHT WERE NORMAL. After all we've been through, you'd think that Jews would all be fearless. But here are five well-known Jews and their lesser-known fears. And you thought *you* were neurotic?

Sid Caesar, a comedian, fear of haircuts; **Sigmund Freud,** father of psychoanalysis, fear of train travel; **David Steinberg**, comedian, fear of snakes; **Jonah Hill**, actor, fear of birds; **Matt Lauer** (Jewish father), fear of vomiting and fear of lightning.

A JEW WHOSE FATHER WAS THE LEADER OF A NOTORIOUS CULT Well-known writer **Neil Gaiman's** father was the head of the weird Scientology "Church" in England. But in England and most countries, they don't call it a Church but a cult. Neil's father, **David Gaiman** was one of the big shots in Scientology in England, harassing authors who tried to tell the truth about how bad Scientology really is. (Read "The Unbreakable Miss Lovely.")

CONVERTS & SHIKSAS

WILL SIMON COWELL BECOME A JEW? And do we care? Music mogul **Simon Cowell,** best known as a talent judge on *American Idol, Britain's Got Talent,* etc., supposedly plans to convert. Although he was brought up as a Catholic, he had a Jewish father, has a Jewish girlfriend, plus a half-Jewish son who was supposedly circumcised. Despite his TV persona, inspiring nicknames like "Judge Dread" and "Sarcastic Simon,", he's a real mensch, who donated £100,000 to "Friends of the IDF." (Israel Defense Forces)

DREW BARRYMORE: SHIKSA IN THE MIKVAH? Drew Barrymore calls herself a shiksa, but she married under a Chuppah (to a Jew, obviously), and is raising her daughter (**Olive**—that's a Jewish name?) to be Jewish. Presumably, she'll do the same for her second child, **Frankie.**

Drew says she plans to remove her six tattoos (whaaa?) in preparation. She says she loves Passover and plans to convert—but she's been saying that for a while. By the time she makes up her mind, it could be time for her to be buried in a Jewish cemetery.

NOT EVERYONE WANTS GWYNETH PALTROW TO CONVERT Gwyneth Paltrow is generally considered Jewish—she's raising her two children, **Apple,** and **Moses** as Jews—but her mother, actress **Blythe Danner,** is a Pennsylvania Dutch Quaker. Her father, producer **Bruce Paltrow** (*White Shadow, St. Elsewhere*), was Jewish.

Gwyneth, who is a follower of Kabbalah, says she is converting. But columnist **Andrea Peyser** in the *New York Post* suggests Gwyneth "join another tribe." Peyser's objection is that Paltrow pushes expensive fad diets on people but "the health-food maven" smokes cigarettes!

FAMOUS SHIKSA WIVES

In 1986, **Caroline Kennedy** married **Ed Schlossberg**. *New York* magazine said: "It should have scandalized her mother, but by then, haute goy **Jackie Kennedy Onassis** had already spent four years with **Maurice Tempelsman,** an orthodox Jewish Yiddish-speaking--presumably not with her--diamond merchant from Antwerp.

In 1997, **Karenna Gore,** daughter of almost-President **Al Gore**, married **Andrew Schiff.** And he was a doctor, leaving one less Jewish doctor for a Jewish girl to aim for. Although the groom's ancestors were a German-Jewish banking family with roots going back to **King Solomon,** he was raised Episcopalian.

NOTE: But we gained a half Jew! JFK's only grandson, **John "Jack" Schlossberg,** 22 in 2015, is at Yale, training to become an emergency medical technician. So not only do we have another half-Jew, but a doctor no less!

Lauren Bush, the niece of **George W.,** and granddaughter of President **George H.W.** and **Barbara Bush,** married designer **Ralph Lauren's** son, **David,** after a seven-year courtship.

Would she have married him if his family name was still **Lifshitz?**

JUST SO YOU SHOULD KNOW

Although he later described himself as an atheist, **Mark Zuckerberg,** founder of Facebook, had a Bar Mitzvah, and the theme was *Star Wars*.

Dr. Ruth was once a sniper in the Haganah, chosen not only because of her fearlessness but her tiny size, which enabled her to easily hide. Ruth's boyfriend was 6-feet tall, and the size disparity (she's 4-feet 7-inches) made it difficult for them to go up on a ski lift T-bar together. One time, when she reached the top, she told him she was going back down with "that short man," and pointed to the 5-foot **Fred Westheimer.** They married less than a year later. Fred sometimes called Ruth "my little skiing accident."

CHAPTER 6

HOW TO WOO A JEW
AND MEET A MENSCH EVEN YOUR
MOTHER WOULD LOVE

⬡

AAAH...MEN

HOT MAMALA'S 10 BEST PLACES TO NAIL A JEWISH
HUSBAND: A long time ago, singles went to Grossinger's and the
Concord, and before that, spent a week at Green Mansions,
Tarleton or Tamarac. Now, according to the book *Hot Mamala,*
the following may be the best places to find a nice Jewish boy or
girl.

Israel Defense Forces, American Israel Public Affairs Committee,
hospitals, Jewish weddings, executive offices of Google, Ben
Gurion Airport, the Miami boardwalk during Passover, the upper
west side [of New York] on Simchat Torah, MBA computer science
or engineering programs, all of Jerusalem, especially during
Passover & Sukkoth.

A TOP JEWISH MATCHMAKER GIVES DATING TIPS
Lisa Ronis isn't your ordinary shadchan. This Syrian-American
Jew has a starting package of $15,000 for a minimum of eight
dates, and her clientele is upscale singles too busy to meet Mr. or
Mrs. Right on his or her own. Here's her advice on how to get
things started.

FOR WOMEN

Don't go out with packs of women. If a guy is alone and wants to talk with you, he won't walk over to a crowd of girls. If he does, while you may be one of the chosen people, you may not be the person chosen.

Don't talk on the phone with him for more than 10 minutes before a first date. Spark his curiosity and leave something for the first date.

Practice flirting on a daily basis. In the grocery store, in an elevator, in line at the airport...think of it as stretching exercises!

Wear something feminine or stylish on a date, but never too sexy. That sends the wrong message.

When you start dating a guy you are just wild about, continue to date several other men as well in order not to focus obsessively on him—or be too heartbroken if it doesn't work out.

FOR MEN

Plan a nice evening. Don't show up and say, "Where should we go?" Women like a man with a plan.

No sneakers allowed on a date unless you are playing tennis, going sailing, or going to the gym.

Don't talk about yourself, your divorce, or your ex-girlfriend all night long.

Always pay for the first few dates.

If you really like her, ask her out on a second date within a couple of days. Keep the romance going, growing, and flowing. Send her gorgeous flowers the next day.

If she has kids, make sure that you ask all about them. Same for dogs and cats.

HOW ONE MAN CHOOSES HIS WIFE

A Jewish matchmaker found what she thought was the perfect mate for one of her clients. He met her but told the matchmaker that unless he saw her naked, he wouldn't consider marriage to her.

When the matchmaker told the girl what he wanted, she protested. Finally, she agreed and reluctantly totally stripped for her hopeful intended.

The next day the matchmaker called the man and said "Well..." (Or "Vel...")"What did you think of her?"

"Forget it," said the man. "I didn't like her nose."

MATCHMAKER, MATCHMAKER DO-IT-YOURSELF—ONLINE

ONLINE PLACES TO MEET YOUR (JEWISH) MATE Figures vary, but many say that as many as one-third of all marriages are now a result of people meeting on the Internet. Many of those matches are direct from online dating services. While match.com and *OKCupid.com* and the others do match up Jewish singles, here are a few sites (and these may change) that specialize in Jewish matchmaking.

Jdate.com, chaiexpectations.com; isawyouatsinai.com (mostly orthodox); coffee meets bagel (app); jswipe (app); jmom (Mothers choosing partners with kids); jcrush.com (swipe right to crush and left to "oy vey.")

A FEW TIPS FOR WRITING A GOOD ONLINE PERSONAL Joanna Rothman, the author of *singlesassy.com*, who helps people with their online profiles, gave a few tips in *Brandeis* magazine.

- **CHOOSE ONE THAT COSTS MONEY** "OK Cupid... very popular [but]you have to weed through a lot of spam. People who pay for online dating tend to take it more seriously." And be less chintzy.
- **KEEP USERNAMES CLASSY** "I've used the username 'Loves2Travel2Europe.'"
- **BE SPECIFIC IN YOUR PROFILE** "...Instead of writing that you enjoy 'travel,' mention a recent trip you've taken...You're more likely to attract the attention of someone who has done the same."
- In the end, she promises: "Soon you'll be engaged, and your mother will be plotzing." From her ears...

☺ HILARIOUS JEWISH PERSONALS

Funnyandjewish.com **has collected Jewish personal ads...**

Yeshiva bochur, Torah scholar, long beard, payos. Seeks same in woman.

Divorced Jewish man, seeks partner to attend shul with, light shabbos candles, celebrate holidays, build Sukkah together, attend brisses, and Bar Mitzvahs. Religion not important.

Jewish Princess, 28, seeks successful businessman of any major Jewish denomination: hundreds, fifties, twenties.

Israeli woman, 28, works behind falafel counter in pizza shop, looking for Jewish man with sense of humus.

Single Jewish woman, 29, into disco, mountain climbing, skiing, track and field. Has slight limp.

Jewish businessman, 49, manufactures Sabbath candles, Chanukah candles, Havdalah candles, Yahrzeit candles. Seeks non-smoker.

Israeli professor, 41, with 18 years of teaching in my behind. Looking for American-born woman who speaks English very good.

CHAPTER 7
JEWISH LIFE [& PETS]

MARRIAGE & JEWISH MOTHERS

FORGET SEX? WHAT ARE THE REAL REASONS THEY BREAK THE GLASS AT WEDDINGS? Who hasn't heard about that glass smashing equaling wedding night performance stuff. But that's just one reason. Some jokingly say that maybe a man smashes the glass because it is the last time he'll be able to foot his foot down.

The comedian, **David Bader**, said: "The groom might break the glass as a reminder to the wedding guests that the couple has registered for new wine glasses."

Seriously, here are the reasons given in *Judaism for Dummies*.

A reminder of the destruction of the temple in Jerusalem.

A reminder that even at times of great joy, things shatter and there's loss.

A symbolic breaking of the old structure to create space for new possibilities.

It's telling us that just as breaking a glass is permanent and irrevocable, so should be the marriage.

And finally, to drive away evil spirits so as not to arouse the evil eye with so much joy and happiness.

THE JEWISH GROUP THAT WANTS MEN TO HAVE MORE THAN ONE WIFE—AT A TIME There is a Jewish group promoting polygamy as a solution to too many women, and also as a way to prevent a married man from cheating. *Reuters* reported that this new Jewish organization, the "brainchild" of **Habayit Hayehudi Hashalem,** even took out an ad in the *Shabbat BeShabato* promoting the concept—and claimed to have received responses from 100 men. (That's all?)

How would a man ever get his (Jewish) wife to accept another one? Author **A. J. Jacobs,** in a hilarious book called *The Year of Living Biblically,* quotes one advocate of multiple wives as suggesting it might work if you "pray like you've prayed only when you're in trouble."

THINGS A JEWISH MOTHER WOULD *NEVER* SAY

Versions of this have been circulating for years, but this one was compiled by **Marney Winston-Macaul** and appeared on *aish.com*.

"Not everybody needs higher education. Hamburger U is good enough, darling."

"It's fine, *mamala*. Go to Las Vegas with your wife. My 65th birthday we can celebrate any year."

"I think a cluttered bedroom is a sign of creativity."

"Oy, I forgot my tissues. Just use your sleeve."

"Try it. Live with him a few years. Then, if it works out, you'll see if you want to marry him."

"About naming the baby after Grandpa Irving, may he rest in peace. If you want to name him Luke Picard Lipchitz instead, that's fine with us."

"Personally, I think the decision to pierce a nose should be up to the individual teenager."

"School isn't everything. The marines are nice."

"If your new wife wants you to move to Hungary to be close to her family, it's fine by us."

"I saw your subscription to *Playboy* was expiring, so I sent a check in to renew it."

"Of course, you can walk to school on your own, *bubbala*. You'll only have to cross three main roads."

CHILDREN

TOP JEWISH CHILDREN'S NAMES IN AMERICA
Kveller.com took the most popular baby names in America in 2012 and figured out which were Jewish. "While some Jewish names are almost exclusively reserved for Jews (we're looking at you, Zev and Dov), there are other names that have made it into the American lexicon." Here they are.

BOYS: 1) Jacob [#1] 2) Noah [#4] 3) Michael [#8]

4) Daniel [#11] 5) Elijah [#13]

GIRLS: 1) Abigail [#7] 2) Elizabeth [#10)] 3) Ella [#12]

4) Hannah [#22] 5) Leah [#33]

BIZARRE BIBLICAL NAMES YOU SHOULD NEVER EVER GIVE YOUR KID

Kveller.com lists some terrible names from the Bible they say you should avoid giving your child.

BOYS: Anani, Kenaniah, Shammuah, Ichabod, Pallu

GIRLS: Abishag, Gomer, Rahab, Zibiah, Hephzibah

MAN OFFERS TO LET ANYONE NAME HIS JEWISH BABY—FOR $20,000 So, there was this man in New Jersey with nine children who named all of them after relatives. But then he ran out of relatives whose names he could use. Unfortunately, he didn't run out of *children,* and when he had a tenth one, he decided to sell the naming rights. Some misogynists on the Internet suggested he sell the girl rather than the name.

Adam Soclof of *jta.org* broke this strange story after he received a tip that someone on Craigslist was offering to sell the naming rights to his daughter—for a minimum of $20,000. The man hoped to sell it to someone who didn't have children or wanted to honor a relative or the memory of someone killed in the Holocaust. "We're a little rushed; we'd like to name the baby on Saturday," the man told him on Thursday.

"Whoever would do this, we would consider them like family," the caller said. He promised to invite the namesake to the bat mitzvah, to the wedding and "say Kaddish for them after 120 years." Wouldn't a new child be likely to outlive *him*?

Would someone really pay to be related to someone like this? We'll never know because the ad was quickly taken down. In the end, the man ended up naming his daughter **Rina,** a Hebrew name meaning Joy.

Perhaps in honor of her parents, she should have been named Meshugenah.

NO JEWISH CHILD WILL EVER GROW UP IN A HOME WITH THESE

In Jewish as a Second Language: How to Worry. How to Interrupt. How to Say the Opposite of What You Mean, Molly Katz tells what you'll never find in a Jewish residence.

Bowling shoes. A painting of kittens with big eyes. Trout flies. Boxing gloves. A poo-poo cushion. A Rottweiler.

JEWISH GEOGRAPHY

THE SEVEN STATES WITH THE *LEAST* AMOUNT OF JEWS Jerry Seinfeld joked that his parents moved to Florida when they were 60. "They didn't want to, but that's the law."

New York is the other state most associated with Jews. As the comedian, **Lenny Bruce** once put it: "Even if you are Catholic, if you live in New York, you're Jewish. If you live in Butte, Montana, you are going to be a goy even if you are Jewish."

Here, alphabetically, are the states with fewer than 2,000 Jews. Arkansas, Idaho, Mississippi, Montana, North Dakota, South Dakota, Wyoming.

WHATEVER HAPPENED TO THE "THE BORSCHT BELT" HOTELS? People once went to the Catskills, fondly known as the "Borscht Belt," to eat and meet, mostly unmarried people of the opposite sex. **Billy Crystal** in *700 Sundays* said that if **Osama bin Laden** had been hiding in the Catskill Mountains, and one of the women came upon him, they would have asked, "Are you single?"

Tania Grossinger, the author of *Growing Up At Grossinger's,* tells what ultimately happened to the great resorts where Jews once vacationed.

GROSSINGER'S: Along with the Concord, this was the most upscale resort in the Catskills. They served 150,000 guests a year and had 35 buildings plus their own post office. They closed in 1986.

THE CONCORD: Closed and now affiliated with Mohegan Sun. They plan to open a hotel and casino there.

NEVELE: This resort, which is eleven spelled backward, is closed, and has been mired in litigation not worth going into.

BROWN'S: which comedian **Jerry Lewis** made famous, and vice versa, was pretty much destroyed in 2012 in a fire so large, they had to call in 43 fire companies and 300 firefighters. It was not a "Jewish fire."

KUTSHER'S: In the old days, basketball star **Wilt Chamberlain** once worked as a bellhop here and supposedly wowed incoming guests by lifting their luggage and tossing them into the second-floor windows. The resort was purchased in 2013 by an Indian billionaire who plans to demolish it and turn it into a health and wellness center. Kosher it won't be.

PETS

ARE JEWS DOG OR CAT PEOPLE? How Jews feel about pets is a complicated question, and the answer depends on which Jews and when. Today, regardless of their religion, most people who own dogs and cats love them—and vice versa. As **Nora Ephron** wrote: "When your children are teenagers, it's important to have a dog so that someone in the house is happy to see you."

But some think that extremely Orthodox people may not have as many pets as other Jews. An Orthodox website, *Jewinthecity.com* points out that many people have dogs in lieu of children—but the Orthodox have children! And more children means more expenses and less space for pets.

Mark Levenson in "Of Canines and Commandments," feels that those who adhere strictly to kosher rules may also find that owning pets can cause complications—especially at Passover. Shabbat, too, can present problems. *Jewfaq.org* claims that "Several sources say that walking a dog is permitted, but if an animal runs away on Shabbat, it is not permitted to trap the animal."

But Levenson cites another reason why Orthodox people, especially older ones, might be dogged by bad feelings toward what others consider their best friends. "From the Crusades to the Pogroms to the Holocaust...[dogs have been] set on them by anti-Semitic persecutors. If Jews have a racial memory of dogs, it's not a happy one."

The mention of dogs is even more negative in the Bible, where, mirroring societal attitudes toward dogs at that time, Jews were viewed and treated like, well, dogs. As **Rabbi Judah Elijah Schochet** points out in *Animal Life in Jewish Tradition*, dogs were described as being noisy [Psalms 59:7-14], greedy [Isaiah 56:11], stupid [Isaiah 56:10], filthy [Proverbs 26:11]. The term "dog" is applied as an insult to humans [I Kings 22:38]. Furthermore, "dog" appears to have been a derogatory designation for male prostitutes [Deuteronomy 23:19].

If the Bible was downright nasty to dogs, were cats viewed any better? Actually, they weren't viewed at all; they simply aren't mentioned. While the Egyptians loved cats and even worshiped one as a goddess, there is no indication that Jews shared the fondness of the Egyptians for cats. For that matter, they didn't care terribly for Egyptians, either.

Still, there is one possibly positive reference to dogs in the Old Testament. As the Jews were leaving Egypt, "...no dog wagged its tongue." Therefore, Jews were able to escape without attracting attention. It may not be saying much to praise creatures only for keeping their mouths shut, but there are probably people we wish we could praise for exactly that.

OK, JEWISH DOGS, YOU CAN UNCROSS YOUR LEGS NOW No one's going to neuter you—maybe It's a violation of Jewish law to neuter your male pet, according to Leviticus, which maintains that you can't castrate a male of any species. As for female pets, technically that doesn't mean you can't spay her, but some think that it's also prohibited by general laws against causing pain to animals. However, you can adopt a dog or cat who has *already* been altered (declawed, or ears and tails docked, all of which are also not permitted), and that's probably the best bet anyway.

Here's another Sabbath rule according to *Judaism101* (at *jewfaq.org*). You can violate the Sabbath a bit to rescue animals in pain or at risk of death. For example, you can move them, give them medicine, or find a shabbos goy to do it. But on the Sabbath, your dogs can't work for you. They're also entitled to rest, so you can't have them fetch your newspaper. This probably doesn't apply to your cat, who isn't going to get your newspaper for you anyway.

HOW TO HAVE A JEWISH DOG OR CAT Should you feed your dog on the Sabbath? Sell your non-kosher dog food to a non-kosher non-Bark-mitzvahed dog?

Rabbi Zvi Goldberg, the Administrator for the kosher certification agency, Star-K, said that a person must feed his animals on Shabbos and Yom Tov if the pet is dependent on him for sustenance. A feral cat, fish in the pond, animals in a zoo, etc., may not be fed, since it is assumed they may find their food elsewhere and feeding them involves unnecessary effort.

Even when feeding is permitted—and they do sell kosher pet food—people must minimize their efforts in feeding their pets. For example, if a dog is fed a large slab of meat, and can eat it without further preparation, the owner must give it to him/her intact. If the dog cannot eat it because it is too large, then the owner may cut it down into smaller portions.

JASON BIGGS HAD A BARK-MITZVAH FOR HIS DOG Some people thought they were barking mad, but when their pup came of age at 13, **Jason Biggs** (not Jewish) and his wife **Jenny Mollen** (Jewish) had a Bark-Mitzvah for their poodle (apparently Jewish). And yes, people have been known to throw Cat-Mitzvahs as well.

The oddball ceremony, which was Instagrammed, was held at the Sinai Temple in Los Angeles, with challah, a candle-lighting ceremony, a yarmulke on their dog, and even a ketubah. If they had owned a cat, would it have been a cat-tuba?

No word on how well the pup did on his Arf-Torah.

PS If you think posting a Bark Mitzvah on Instagram is a bit too much, you should see the photos and comments they posted on their son's circumcision. Or better you shouldn't see them.

TOYS FOR FOUR-LEGGED TOTS

TOYS YOU CAN BUY YOUR JAP (JEWISH AMERICAN PUPPY) Many shops and websites with names like *oytoys.com,* *moderntribe.com, jewishsource.com* sell the following.

FOR DOGS: T-shirt saying JAP (Jewish American puppy), dog bowls saying "meshugenah dog," (T-shirt with pix of doxie) "My wiener is 100% kosher," a stuffed pig that says "treif" on it, scissors saying "moyel" on it.

AND FOR CATS: A catnip coin saying "gelt," a catnip dreidel, a catnip fish saying "lox."

WILL A "YAMACLAUS" MAKE YOUR DOG LOOK TOO JEWISH?

Merry Canine Christmas! For doggies from mixed marriages, buy them a "Yamaclaus" so they can celebrate Christmas as well as Hanukkah. A Yamaclaus is a red yarmulke with a white furry border around it like a Santa outfit. You have to see it to (dis)believe it.

Here's a dog wearing a yamaclaus, on a fun site called *hipsterjew.com.*

💻www.hipsterjew.com/wp-content/uploads/2012/12/ yama_paws-450x450.jpg

---

JUST SO YOU SHOULD KNOW

Sarah Palin, American tea party politician and almost Vice President of the US under almost-President **John McCain,** has a dog named Hadassa. [*Sic*]

"Did My Dog Learn Anything From Eating My Tefillin?" was the headline of an actual story in *virtualjerusalem.com.*

David Ben-Gurion, who was the first Prime Minister of Israel, came to Palestine as a farm worker when he was 20 years old and fed animals before he entered politics.

Although actor **Christopher Walken's** father was Jewish, he converted to marry Christopher's mother. When Christopher was 15 years old, he joined a traveling circus and trained as a lion tamer.

CHAPTER 8
SPORTS

OLYMPICS

SHOULD OLYMPIC SKATERS PERFORM TO THE THEME FROM *SCHINDLER'S LIST?* The subject of skaters dancing to *Schindler*...came up after **Julia Lipnitskaya**, representing a country notorious for its anti-Semitism (Russia), danced to the *Schindler* theme song during the last Olympics. The reported reaction of most Jews was to feel more frozen than chosen.

Daniel D'Addario, a staff reporter for *Salon's* entertainment section said sarcastically: "I think I speak for all of us when I say, 'Finally, someone has adapted the saddest scene from a Holocaust movie into an acrobatic figure-skating routine.'"

D'Addario complained that dancing to *Schindler* was "a low-calorie emotional trigger...introducing the memories of another little girl's tragic fate is unsporting.... It weighs the scale in her favor unduly. Who wants to be the one to root against the [Holocaust victim]?.... Not to mention that it's using someone else's tragedy for her hoped-for personal gain."

ARAB OLYMPIC STARS REPRESENTING ISRAEL—NOT SO MANY... NOT SO SURPRISING Out of 338 athletes who have represented Israel in the 19 Olympics games, only two were Arab athletes, in soccer and weightlifting. And the last time was in 1976.

As one poster on *Quora.com* said: "And how much do you think they will offer for a head of an Arab athlete who won something for Israel? I guess no Israeli Arab wants to find out."

BASEBALL

GREAT MOMENTS IN BASEBALL HISTORY—WHEN THEY DIDN'T PLAY What was so unique—and memorable— about two famous Jewish baseball players was not the games they played but the ones they *didn't* play. For example, while Los Angeles Dodgers pitcher **Sandy Koufax** regularly played on the Sabbath, he refused to play the first game of the 1965 World Series against the Minnesota Twins on Yom Kippur. The Twins won.

Earlier, **Hank Greenberg**, another famous Jewish baseball player, while non-observant, refused to play for the Detroit Tigers on Yom Kippur in 1934. Without him, they lost to the New York Yankees, 5-2.

THE "BRAINIEST GUY IN BASEBALL" WAS A JEW — WHY IS THAT NOT A SURPRISE? PLUS, HE WAS A SPY; THAT'S A SURPRISE. Moe Berg not only played 15 seasons as a backup catcher in the major leagues during the 20's and 30's-- although he wasn't so hot a player--but he spied for America during the war and later did some work for the CIA.

Smart? He graduated from Princeton and Columbia Law School, read 10 newspapers a day, and won a radio quiz show when he correctly answered questions about the derivation of Latin and Greek words. But he wasn't that smart when it came to business and lived off others for his last 20 years. He died at 70 and was buried in Israel. His final words were: "How did the Mets do today?" Without him, probably quite well.

BOXING

WHY BOXERS TODAY HAVE SHORT HAIR Maybe Delilah was right after all. Remember the story of **Samson and Delilah?** Samson, shorn of his long locks by Delilah's connivance, lost all his strength, and was easily defeated and captured by the Philistines. However, at least one other mighty warrior would have been better off if he had had short hair to begin with—or no hair—like today's boxers.

The shorn look dates back to the early days of boxing in England when between 1792 and 1795, a Jewish man named **Daniel**

Mendoza became the Heavyweight Champion of England.

This 5'7"160-pounder, credited as the father of modern boxing, introduced a more modern style than having two lugs simply stand face-to-face and beat on each other until one fell down. His strategy was avoiding punches by "side-stepping."

But he also introduced something beyond today's "scientific method" of boxing, as is generally attributed to him. While Mendoza was long on brains, and on brawn, he was also long on hair.

On one occasion, his opponent, **"Gentleman" John Jackson**, simply grabbed Mendoza by his hair and pummeled him in the face senseless in a ten-minute rout. While one doubts this strategy would pass muster under the **Marquess of Queensberry** rules, it did then, and since that date, boxers have long worn their hair short.

THE STRANGE STORY OF BOXER BARNEY ROSS
Another Jewish athlete who bucked the stereotype was **Barney Ross,** born in 1909 as **Dov-Ber David Rosofsky.** He wanted to be a Talmudic scholar, but circumstances forced him to be tough. As a teen, he witnessed the brutal murder of his father, a grocer, who was shot resisting a robbery of his store. His mother soon had a nervous breakdown and his younger siblings were sent to an orphanage. He was left to fend for himself and became, basically, a local tough, even working for **Al Capone**.

Never knocked out in his career, he was one of the few boxers to hold titles in three separate weight divisions: lightweight, light welterweight and welterweight. When World War II arrived, he signed up for the military, and unlike most superstar athletes who had merely ceremonial roles, he insisted on fighting. That almost ended when he punched the lights out of a dunce of an officer foolish enough to make an anti-Semitic remark in his presence.

Still, in the aftermath, he went to fight on Guadalcanal. Trapped with incapacitated fellow soldiers, he single-handedly wiped out nearly two dozen Japanese soldiers in an all-night fight, earning a Silver Star and a Presidential Citation from **Franklin Delano Roosevelt**.

UNEXPECTED SPORTS...
UNEXPECTED PLAYERS

NON-TRADITIONAL SPORTS—LIKE WORLD-CHAMPIONSHIP DREIDEL SPINNING It has been said that there comes a point in every Jewish boy's life when he realizes that he's more likely to own a sports team than play for one. But that doesn't stop Jews from taking part, and excelling in some non-traditional sports. Here are a few.

WORLD CHAMPION DREIDEL SPINNER-- Seriously. *Thrillist.com* reported on dreidel championships, whose competitors took on titles like "Oscar de la Menorah," and "Spindiana Jones." They decided who went first with a "gelt flip," and then saw how long their dreidel could last inside "a walled, Star of David-shaped battleground called a 'spinagogue.'"

The best-recorded spin lasted almost 18 seconds, although a Jewish astronaut, **David Wolf,** beat them all in an unofficial game. He was in space during Hanukkah, and zero gravity enabled him to spin a dreidel seemingly endlessly. Eventually, he got tired, and the dreidel floated off—only to have it turn up in an air filter in the capsule weeks after it was back on the ground. But before it went off on its own in space, he kept it going for almost an hour and a half. Now *that's* dreidel spinning!

THAI BOXING A 20-year-old Israeli woman won the Women's World Thai Boxing championship in Thailand. **Sarah Avraham** was a Hindu born in India, but converted when she immigrated to Israel. She began training professionally in a sport called "the art of eight weapons" using fists, elbows, knees, shin, and feet. Indeed, Wikipedia lists eight different ways to strike with one's elbow, nine different ways to kick, eight moves with your knee, five-foot thrusts, and more. *Ouch.*

WINDSURFING Gal Fridman is the only Israeli athlete to win two Olympic medals and also the first Olympic gold medalist in Israeli history. Plus, he also won the Israeli Cycling Championship. Sadly, the only medal he still has is the gold one since the rest were stolen from his parents' home after a robbery.

SURPRISE—FOUR JEWS YOU WOULDN'T EXPECT TO BE INTO SPORTS

Patrick Swayze, who was the sexy star of the "Jewish movie" *Dirty Dancing,* (and according to *Wiki Answers* was most likely born Jewish), hoped to go to college on a football scholarship. The night the scouts came to check his team out, he got his left leg nearly snapped in half at the knee, and that ended his football career. But fortunately not his dancing.

Swayze was also a good fighter. According to *The New York Daily News,* he got jumped by five bullies in high school. Afterward, Swayze's father got the school coach to separate the boys, and Patrick boxed each one-by-one and beat them all.

Comedian **Jon Stewart** was on the soccer team when he went to William & Mary College.

Singer **Neil Diamond** went to New York University on a fencing scholarship.

Madeleine Albright, a Jewish former Secretary of State, who proudly talks about her exercise program and what good shape she's in, claims to be able to leg press 400 pounds.

THE FIRST MARATHON RUNNER WAS JEWISH—NOT GREEK Only those of you who really know your Bible, or your sports, know that a Jew ran a marathon hundreds of years before the Greeks ever thought of it. And typically, the Jew got no credit for it. Nobody even remembers his name. But the Greek **Pheidippides,** who ran from Marathon to Athens, was forever "remembered" with the name "Marathon."

Even before Pheidippides' fateful flight, however, one Biblical Hebrew made a similar run, also to transmit news of a battle. Unlike the Greeks, who ran to announce that they had been victorious, the Hebrews brought dreadful, depressing news. (Like your mother often does.)

Thirty thousand Israeli footmen had been slain, and if that wasn't enough of a bummer, "the Ark of God was taken." Pheidippides died after delivering his message. But the enterprising "man of Benjamin" unintentionally killed the recipient, **Eli the High Priest**! Upon hearing the tragic news, Eli "fell from off the seat backward by the side of the gate, and his neck broke, and he died."

The kicker to this tale, according to *haaretz.com*, is that in 1968, when the founder of the Israeli Olympic Committee actually measured this Benjamin guy's run, supposedly, it turned out to be the same length of a marathon: 42 kilometers. So instead of Olympics, it's been suggested that it should have been called the "Man of Benjamin" run.

PREJUDICE AGAINST ATHLETES

HOW TWO JEWISH SPORTS HEROES HANDLED HATERS AND HECKLERS All major Jewish athletes have had problems with anti-Semitism, but you can imagine what the first Arab soccer player on the Israeli national team, went through several decades ago when he played.

An article in *haaretz.com* quoted **Rifaat (Jimmy) Tourk**, the **"Jackie Robinson of Israeli soccer,"** as saying that when he neared the stands, so much spit was catapulted down on him that he often felt like it was raining! But he got his revenge. He said that when rival players would taunt him, he'd say nothing. But during the game, there might be "an unavoidable collision, an accident…"

Famed baseball player, **Hank Greenberg**, also had problems with being Jewish. According to *The Complete Idiot's Guide to Jewish History & Culture:* "Every SOB was calling me names, so I had to make good. As time went by, I came to feel that if I, as a Jew, hit a home run, I was hitting one against **Hitler**," he said after hitting 58 home runs in the 1938 season.

THE RABBI WHO'S FRIENDS WITH THE POPE: Before he became **Pope Francis, Jorge Mario Bergoglio** was extremely good friends with **Rabbi Abraham Skorka**. The Rabbi, like the Pope, was also a soccer nut. The Rabbi told *60 Minutes* that the two once played on competing teams, and the Rabbi's team often lost. So the Pope jokingly liked to refer to the Rabbi's team as the "Chickens." Before the games, the future Pope used to like to tell the Rabbi: "I guess we're going to eat chicken soup."

ARE THESE JEWISH SPORTS MASCOTS OFFENSIVE? Comedian **Elayne Boosler** joked that while some Native Americans find football names ("Redskins," etc.,) odious, Jews wouldn't be offended if the Atlanta Braves were called "The Atlanta Bravermans" or the Chicago White Sox were called "The Chicago White Socks with Sandals."

Along the same line, **Sam Greenspan** in *11points.com*, wrote: "When I was growing up, and a teacher wanted to make a point about offensive mascots, she'd always say, 'How would you feel if a team was called the 'Fightin' Jews' and the mascot had a hook nose and a bagel?' We were supposed to be deeply offended, but I wasn't. I wished that someone would think the Jews were tough and frightening enough to name their team after us. And not their legal defense team, their football team."

JUST SO YOU SHOULD KNOW

David Beckham, the famous soccer player's maternal grandmother is Jewish; according to *jewage.org*. Beckham has referred to himself as "half Jewish," and spoken of the influence the religion has had on him.

There's a famous "sports" story, reprinted in *imdb.com,* about **Peter Falk,** who was best known for his role in an old TV hit called *Columbo.* As a result of a childhood disease, Falk had a glass eye. When he was playing in a Little League game, the umpire called him out. Falk disagreed with the call, pulled his glass eye out of its socket, and handed it to the umpire. "Here, I think you might need this."

Comedian and actor **Billy Crystal** is obsessed with baseball and the Yankees. For his 60th birthday, on March 12, 2008, his beloved Yankees signed him to a contract as a gift. He had one at-bat and struck out against the Pittsburgh Pirates during an exhibition game.

The most famous sportscaster of his generation, **Howard Cosell,** was the grandson of a rabbi and was born as **Howard Cohen.**

The first professional baseball player was a Jew named **Emanuel Pike,** who played in the mid-1880's—for $20 a week.

There's a video "Every Jewish and Israeli Olympic Champion Since the 1972 Massacre"...not surprisingly it's only 2 & 1/2 minutes long.

www.jewsnews.co.il/2014/02/20/every-jewish-and-israeli-olympic-champion-since-the-72-munich-massacre/

CHAPTER 9
HANUKKAH & CHRISTMAS

HANUKKAH

MERRY CHRISTMUKKAH! According to *Hanukkah in America,* more non-Jews than Jews approved of putting a menorah up in a public place! Four-fifths of white non-Jews in America favored it and three-fifths of blacks did. But only one-third of American Jews did, according to a survey by the National Council of Jewish Women.

FOUR THINGS YOU MAY NOT KNOW ABOUT HANUKKAH

- There is no mention of Hanukkah in the Old Testament.
- In New Orleans, some decorate their doors with menorahs made of hominy grits. (Isn't that a bit messy?)
- Latkes in Texas are seasoned with cilantro and cayenne pepper.
- Ethiopian Jews break all of their dishes and make new ones to symbolize a complete break from the past and a new start.

THE SECOND MOST IMPORTANT QUESTION PEOPLE ASK ABOUT HANUKKAH The most common question is probably how to spell the holiday. (Chanukah, Chanukkah, Chanukka, Channukah, Hanukah, or Hannukah?) But the next most common question is most likely how to get the wax off the menorah. *Tabletmag.com* asked their readers to give tips.

- Freeze the menorah—and the wax will pop off.

- Fill the sink with hot water and put the menorah in. Or pour hot water over the outside to make it easier to clean later.

- Before inserting a candle, spray the openings with something like Pam.

- Freeze the candles before using them.

- Buy dripless candles. Kosher. Made in Israel. (Available at *amazon.com*)

CHRISTMAS

WHY DO JEWISH PEOPLE EAT CHINESE FOOD AT CHRISTMAS? And anytime as well. A Jewish kid was overheard at his school Christmas choral contest singing the song "God Rest Ye Merry Gentlemen" as "God Rest You Jerry Mandelbaum," reflecting how Jewish Christmas has become for so many.

And what could be more Jewish than eating Chinese food during Christmas? Surely, you've heard the joke about the Jewish culture being established before the Chinese one, so where did Jews then eat? Or that a famous Jewish leader was Genghis Cohen, not **Genghis Khan**?

But Jews eating Chinese food—especially at Christmas—isn't a joke. It's almost a Commandment. So what exactly is it with Jews and Chinese food?

For starters, the cuisines, as different as they seem, actually share a lot of the same flavors: sweet and sour, lots of garlic and onions, etc. Also, the Chinese don't usually mix dairy and meat, perhaps because there isn't that much dairy in their dishes anyway.

Jewish comedians joke that Jewish dietary laws only allow Jews to eat pork and shellfish in a Chinese restaurant. That also isn't entirely a joke, because not-so-religious Jews who would still rather not eat pork or shellfish can eat it in a Chinese restaurant without really seeing what it is. Pork and shrimp don't look all that obvious or forbidden when they're all chopped up and battered.

Some Chinese realize they've got a good thing going by attracting a Jewish clientele. A few Chinese restaurants have even named menu items in a way to tempt Jews. Like one listing wonton soup on the menu as "Chicken soup with kreplach"—which isn't inaccurate. Another served "Lo Mein Bernstein" prepared with something they thought Jews would like: chicken livers. Kosher Chinese restaurants in Manhattan have given themselves names like Shang-Chai, and Moshe Peking, where the Chinese waiters wore yarmulkes.

Finally, though, there's an often over-looked non-religious reason so many Jews go to Chinese restaurants at Christmas. Unlike Christians who traditionally have a large home-cooked meal with their family that day, Jews save their feast for their own holidays, like Passover. Thus, Jews often go to eat out that night, and Chinese restaurants, unlike so many other places owned by Christians are actually open on Christmas.

THE NINE BEST JEWISH MOVIES TO WATCH AT CHRISTMAS Paul Noble, winner of 5 Emmys and former host of a TV show on Fox on old movies, gives his list of the nine best Jewish movies to watch at Christmas so you don't have to watch *It's a Wonderful Life* for the fiftieth time.

The Boy in the Striped Pajamas, Schindler's List, Annie Hall, The Chosen, Everything is Illuminated, Exodus, Fiddler on the Roof, Marjorie Morningstar, An American Tail.

HANUKKAH EXPLAINED BY CHRISTIANS

⌨www.unitedwithisrael.org/watch-chanukah-explained- by-christians/

CHRISTMAS EXPLAINED BY JEWS Not as funny as the above, but hey, equal time.

⌨http://tinyurl.com/oukadcp

JUST SO YOU SHOULD KNOW

Adam Sandler's "Hanukkah Song" sounds better when it's sung by **Neil Diamond,** and the video is more interesting too. http://tinyurl.com/putlt5j

More Jews have Christmas trees (1 in 3) than have kosher kitchens.

Remember the *Seinfeld* episode in which George's father, Frank Costanza suggested a holiday called "Festivus" (for the rest of us) in lieu of Christmas and Hanukkah? It was actually created decades earlier by a writer named **Dan O'Keefe** to celebrate his wife's anniversary. His son was a writer of *Seinfeld,* which is how it got there.

CHAPTER 10
PASSOVER

DON'T PASS OVER THESE

IS MARIJUANA KOSHER FOR PASSOVER? In the category of "in case you want to know"—we won't ask why—Israel's Green Leaf Party, which supports marijuana legalization, says you can't smoke pot during Passover, or even have it around, because hemp seeds are forbidden for Passover. *(kitniyot).* So the phrase "High Holidays" obviously does not refer to this one.

Anne Cohen, writing in a blog in the *forward.com,* explains that while Biblical laws only prohibit eating leavened foods, rabbis have included beans, corn and rice in this. Hemp seeds, found in marijuana, are in that category. But wait, that's for the Ashkenazis. Sephardic Jews traditionally do eat kitniyot during Passover.

Medical marijuana is another story. In fact, an Israeli company called Cannabliss, that supplies medical marijuana to Hadassah hospital has made kosher for Passover Pot Cookies. Cohen concludes, "As the ancients said: 'Put that in your pipe and smoke it.' But don't. Still not kosher."

WHY SOME MONKEYS BECAME FAT & LAZY AROUND PASSOVERS Well, I'll be a monkey's Uncle! Zookeepers and visitors began to wonder why monkeys were getting fatter and, therefore, lazier in New York around Passover time. Obviously, no one was inviting them to a Seder, nor were they surreptitiously sipping the wine meant for Elijah. What kind of monkey business was going on?

And then someone figured it out. **Carol Vinzant**, writing in *New York* magazine, revealed that they realized Jews were behind it. (So what else is new?) Before Passover, Jews get rid of all hametz. And who wants to throw away perfectly good food? Certainly not us.

Thus, people started monkeying around with the simians. They took their hametz to the zoos and tossed it to the monkeys, filling and fattening them up. So then they didn't eat the healthy monkey food. Incidentally, the Snow monkeys were a favorite for the food tossers? No ? Vinzant wrote that the polar bear's glass wall was too high, "and the sea lions would only be interested if offered gefilte fish."

The staff was warned to be on the lookout for "suspicious packages of cookies, pretzels, hot-dog buns, and pound cake." Probably also payeses and black coats.

Fortunately, most people did stop when they were caught, except for one person who said: "I don't answer to you; I answer to a higher power."

IS IT TRUE THAT JEWISH MEN DIE AFTER PASSOVER?
A few studies have shown that old people die after major holidays, especially Yom Kippur. The date gives them a goal or a reason to keep going. So a study reported in the prestigious British medical journal *The Lancet* claiming to find that Jewish men (not women) tended to die less before Passover, and in dramatic numbers after it, wasn't really surprising.

Their theory as to why it happened, though, was. The explanation the two (non-Jewish) authors came up was something only people who have probably never been through a Passover Seder would give. They thought that since the oldest man leads in the retelling of the story of Exodus, that's important enough for him to stay alive to do it. Really? Is that something to live for?

Wouldn't overeating at the Seder, with fatty foods like chopped liver before—and too much schnapps afterward—be a more likely culprit after a huge (fatty) meal? Next thing you know, people who know nothing will speculate that Jewish men will themselves to live because they're looking forward to reclining at the seder. Pul-eeze.

Anyway, before you start worrying about what will happen to you or the men in your life after Passover, other (boring) studies have found the opposite. Bottom line: people might die and they might live after Passover. Many Jews believe that's decided only by the determination of God at Yom Kippur. And if you're on the fence about attending a Seder, you might as well go. Don't overeat, and the holiday (probably) isn't gonna kill you. And you can always hope the study is true that the advent of Passover might even help you live a little longer.

WHERE'S THE EXODUS? THE TOP DESTINATION FOR ISRAELIS TO TRAVEL TO DURING PASSOVER Over a million people pass through Ben Gurion Airport during Passover to go to visit family and friends. What was the top choice a few years ago for those leaving Israel for the holiday? Turkey. The follow-up destinations were Crete, Rome, and Bulgaria.

THE SEDER

CHEW ON THIS ONE: THE LAST SUPPER MAY NOT HAVE BEEN A PASSOVER SEDER *Don't Know Much About the Bible* questions whether the last supper was really a Seder. They point out that in most depictions, such as **Leonardo da Vinci's** iconic painting, men were seated around a low table, and no women were present. Some believe that made it unlikely to have been a Seder, since it would have been customary to include women at the meal. Weren't there women at your Seder? On the other hand, an orthodox Seder would probably not have women at the table.

In addition to the lack of women, probably making it a very quiet dinner, there were no traditional edibles there, like Passover lamb and herbs. The first three Gospels state that it was indeed a Passover meal, but the Book of John makes it seem that it was not. So nu?

IS THE WICKED SON REALLY WICKED—OR THE BEST ONE? Every year, when the fathers get to the part at the Seder about the four sons, some of the children at the table secretly start squirming when they get to the part about the wicked son, suspecting their fathers may be addressing them.

But **Joyce Eisenberg** and **Ellen Scolnic** write: "How dare anyone call one of the kids simple! He just has learning differences.... [W]hen we looked around the table we saw one child Googling to find out what animal a shank bone comes from. Another was texting that the matzo balls are sinkers. The youngest was posting selfies...."

So maybe they're not so dumb after all. If you suspect the simple one is you, you can continue to check your Smartphone under the table. Because if you are the "wicked one," maybe that isn't so bad.

The Biblical reason given for why this son (you?) is wicked is he (you?) has separated himself from Jewish tradition. (OK, put aside that Smartphone and focus on the seder.) He's wicked because he's basically asking what this event is all about as if he wasn't part of it.

But *slate.com* has a different take on it. Isn't it a good thing to wonder what a tradition means? Doesn't someone who actually understands something and still does it have a more solid basis for doing it than someone who simply does it because it's "tradition?" Is it "wicked" to ask something that may be a thoughtful exploration of faith? Isn't it part of Jewish culture to challenge authority and question one's beliefs?

Of course. Now put away your cell phone and act interested in what's going on. Then maybe others will stop looking at you sideways when they talk about the "wicked" child.

WEIRD PASSOVER SEDER TRADITIONS According to *thedailymeal.com,* in Gibraltar, they add a bit of brick dust—reminiscent of the mortar the Jews used when building—to the haroseth. There's "much joking about who gets the bit of brick stuck in their tooth," said one guest who ate this odd dish.

In parts of North Africa, there's a custom that the person leading the Seder sometimes walks around with the Seder plate three times when he gets to the part "we left Egypt in haste..." While walking, he also taps the plate on the head of each diner. Someone who witnessed this commented that the kids who were present loved it, but no word on how the adults at the table felt about being bopped on the bean.

In Persia and Afghanistan, the diners may lightly whip each other on the back or shoulder when singing "Dayenu" to symbolize how the slaves were treated. Fortunately, they do it with scallions.

In Hungary, some people put their gold and silver jewelry in the center of the table, symbolizing what happened during the rapid exodus of Jews from Egypt. Hopefully, they remember to take the jewelry home afterward.

PASSOVER HAIKU

David M. Bader has written some very funny Jewish-themed books, including *Haikus for Jews: For You, A Little Wisdom*. Here's the Passover one.

> Left the door open
> for the prophet Elijah.
> Now our cat is gone.

💻THESE WEBSITES WILL GIVE YOU SOMETHING TO TALK OR SING ABOUT AT YOUR SEDER

www.haruth.com/jhumor/JhumorPesach.html

DAYENU: PIECE OF MATZO THAT REALLY LOOKS LIKE ISRAEL

www.imgur.com/r/Israel/WbTI068

JAPANESE VIDEO ON HOW TO BREAK A MATZO IN HALF

http://tinyurl.com/csxbjv

PEOPLE WHO WENT TO A SEDER — OR DID NOT GO

THE NIGHT MARLON BRANDO WENT TO A SEDER Marlon Brando once got an offer he couldn't refuse from his old friend **Louis Kemp**: come to a Seder with him. "I've always wanted to attend a Seder," said Brando, who arrived at the shul with his friend, Native American activist **Dennis Banks,** who came in full buckskin regalia, right down to the feather in his braids. And another famous person at the table was the *normal* guest: **Bob Dylan**.

Brando didn't just watch—and recline either. After the Rabbi invited Brando to deliver a passage from the Haggadah, Brando "stood up and delivered the passage from the Haggadah as if he were reading Shakespeare on Broadway," Kemp recalled in an article for *The Jerusalem Post (jpost.com)*.

Twenty years later, Brando called his old friend Louis and reminisced about the Seder. "I want you to know that I still think about it to this very day," Brando told Kemp. Brando "continued to thank me and tell me of the special spiritual impact it had on him, and how much he identified with a people freeing themselves from bondage and uniting to celebrate and remember that freedom."

MAN MISSES BOTH OF HIS MOM'S SEDERS TO PLAY POKER...WINS $1 MILLION DOLLARS A 45-year old Montreal importer, who played poker for fun, apparently didn't consider Seders as much fun. He went to his mother's home in Florida for Passover, and while he was there, went to play in a poker tournament. And won 1 million dollars.

He told the *Sun-Sentinel* that he considered quitting the tournament as he was advancing (good boy) but didn't (bad). But

86   Was Elvis Jewish?

at least he felt bad about blowing off the dinners. "Here I was moving up the ladder in a big poker tournament, yet I kept getting more depressed," **Eric Afriat** admitted. "I was so sad I thought about just leaving my chips at the table Monday night and going home. But I'm now delighted."

Still, while he may have missed many prayers at the Seder table, he probably prayed a lot at his gaming table, because it's been said that there's no such thing as an atheist in a high-stakes poker game.

✡ ✡ ✡

THE PLAGUES

AN EGYPTIAN IS IN SUCH A CONNIPTION OVER THE 10 PLAGUES THAT HE'S SUING ISRAEL OVER THEM! Some people will sue for anything. **Ahmad al-Gamal**, an Egyptian had a conniption over the 10 plagues. Ahmad complained that **Moses** and the fleeing Jews took certain materials, like gold, silver, and precious stones to build the Tabernacle.

As odd as this charge is, recently, another Egyptian, an academic, made a similar claim. According to *The Jerusalem Post (jpost.com)* this second more recent claim, broadcast on Egyptian TV, was that Jews had "plundered his country all the time—beginning with the theft of Egypt's gold in the days of **Moses**..." He not only demanded that they "return the treasures they stole from us," but also "the interest they denied the Egyptian economy for many decades."

Israel is not the only target. The first guy also wants compensation from the *Ottoman Empire*—which no longer even exists. Plus Britain, for *their* occupation of Egypt. Perhaps the Queen will pony up some gelt for him?

It's surely not necessary. Were it ever brought to court, it would be summarily dismissed. The statute of limitations expired thousands of years ago, since the plagues were probably around 3300 years ago, give or take a century. Not to mention that Ahmad is apparently unfamiliar with the legal doctrine of "Acts of God."

MAYBE THE PLAGUES REALLY DID HAPPEN Every year we hear the story of the plagues, where Moses turned the King's life into a nightmare with the help of a few far-fetched miracles. Rivers of blood, frogs, lice, locusts, flies, boils, dead livestock, thunder and hail, darkness, and the plague that broke the Pharaoh's back, the deaths of the firstborn males.

The story does sound a bit way out—but maybe it isn't. It was widely reported a few years ago that some historians declared that the Biblical Pharaoh really existed and was **Ramesses II**. Furthermore, bizarre events happened around his reign, lending a natural and somewhat plausible explanation for what sounds like a myth or a metaphor.

For instance, the *UK Telegram* reported that **Augusto Mangini,** a paleoclimatologist at the University of Heidelberg indicated that the climate took a serious downturn around when Ramesses II was running the show. That might have dried up the Nile, which could have then become muddy, and the red color made people think the water had turned into blood. Or maybe the dried up river became contaminated with toxic water algae called "blood algae," which can literally turn the water red.

A water ecologist at the Leibniz Institute says this blood algae might have driven all the frogs (*or crocodiles, see below*) out of the Nile, causing them to overrun Egypt. And another biologist at the same Institute reminded us that insects often carry diseases like malaria. "So the next step in the chain reaction is the outbreak of epidemics, causing the human population to fall ill."

We don't know the time frame for all these events, but one of the largest volcanoes in recorded history, Thera, exploded in 1630 BC. That is around the time some say the Exodus occurred, and that could have explained some of the other "miracles," like thunder and darkness.

Finally, we come to the death of the firstborn or eldest male child.

You'd think this sounds pretty selective, pure wrath of God or **Cecil B. DeMille**-type stuff. After all, why not women or the *second* child? But another German scientist (why are all these Germans studying this?) says that a fungus may have polluted the crops. And since the firstborn sons got first dibs on food, they were the first to go.

Of course, some people will continue to believe that God alone did it all, and that's fine too. As **Dr. Robert Miller**, Associate Professor of the Old Testament at The Catholic University of America (at last, an American) said, "I'm reluctant to come up with natural causes for all of the plagues. The whole point was that you didn't come out of Egypt by natural causes, you came out by the hand of God."

WAS THE PLAGUE OF FROGS A CROCK? When you think about it, the second calamity God inflicted on the Egyptians—a plague of frogs—wasn't so bad. Many people think the little critters are kinda cute, and besides, they're beneficial because they eat flies. Now it's not a serious enough problem to make one croak, but there are those who think the second plague was not one of cute frogs but terrifying crocodiles.

Some have argued that "frogs" was a weird word that could have been mistranslated. Most likely not, but if one day your latest Haggadah says the plague was one of crocodiles, it's not worth shedding any crocodile tears over it.

HAMETZ & MATZOS

WHAT'S OK FOR PASSOVER—FOR YOUR DOG? If you have a dog or cat, the kosher certification agency, Star-K (*star-k.org*) publishes a list of acceptable products. But you don't necessarily have to throw the others away. There are people who have "sold" their pet food containing the above to a nonobservant friend and "bought" it back afterward. As **Rabbi Ayelet S. Cohen** said: "The food doesn't belong to you; it just lives in your house during Passover."

Wrote one person on the Internet: "It doesn't matter if you sell your dog food, you still shouldn't feed it to your dog because you are benefiting from hametz. Same with someone else feeding it hametz—you benefit because hametz is being used to maintain your property, the dog. If you sell the dog, that's different."

NOTE: The easiest way to know what to buy, Petco and PetSmart may sell kosher for Passover pet food.

NOW YOU CAN SELL YOUR HAMETZ ONLINE Before Passover, observant Jews get rid of all hametz (leavened products), sometimes by "selling" it to a non-Jew. These days, though, why go looking in your neighborhood for non-Jews especially if you live in places like South Dakota. Just look on the Internet at *chabad.org*. You can sell your leavened products there—and trust that there will be a goy behind the scenes to "buy" it.

CHAPTER 11
PRAYS WELL WITH OTHERS

SERMONS & PRAYERS

HOW TO TALK LIKE A RABBI DURING A SERMON *The Big Jewish Book for Jews* by **Ellis Weiner** and **Barbara Davilman** has some funny chapters, like "How To Purchase, Make And Serve Too Much Food," and "Learn To Whisper So That Everyone Can Hear You (and Then Deny That You Said Anything.")

Here are a few excerpts from their hilarious chapter titled "How to Talk like a Rabbi in 1952."

- "**Quote Maimonides** in your sermons even though no one has the slightest idea who he was."

- "**Lovingly dwell on and thoroughly lay out every thought no matter how potentially small, tangential or obvious.** For example, instead of saying 'Everyone loves hot dogs,' say 'It is an indisputable fact, confirmable through even the most cursory examination of popular literature, as well as via consultation with our own personal experiences.... (blah blah)."

- "**...Rabbinical style:** something that feels to the listener like it must be going somewhere worthwhile and yet is inevitably disappointing when it arrives. If it ever does arrive..."

- "**Pretend to have a sense of humor.** Your joke or anecdotes should go on at length and thus seem like it's going to end in a revelation about the human condition... your joke or anecdote should in no way be the least bit funny. But it should end with what is obviously supposed to be a punch line in order to cue a wry chuckle of recognition from whoever is still awake..."

THE SHEMA Weiner and **Davilman,** in the same hilarious book, also point out that the Shema, the prayer from Deuteronomy, is redundant. "If He's 'the Lord,' then he is automatically 'our God.' It would be like saying, 'Hear O Israel, Doctor Sheldon Greenberg, our primary care doctor, is my primary-care physician.'"

THE RABBI'S MOTHER

Jewish women are boasting about their sons.

"My son is a doctor," says one.

"My son is a lawyer," says the other.

"My son is a rabbi," says the third.

"Rabbi?" the two ask in disbelief. "What kind of job is that for a Jewish boy?"

STUDIES SHOW PRAYER REDUCES ALZHEIMER'S An American-Israeli study reported that praying regularly can reduce the risk of developing Alzheimer's by 50%. This National Institutes of Health study found the protective power of prayer to be especially true for women, who already have a higher chance of developing dementia. Praying didn't necessarily mean going to temple to do it. People who prayed privately showed the same result.

Why would prayer help? Many studies have shown prayer to lower stress levels, which is one of the risk factors for Alzheimer's. Actually, so is sex, but no one has done a study to see whether people with more sex have less Alzheimer's. So you may want to test this yourself at home. Definitely not in a synagogue.

YOU CAN PLACE A PRAYER IN THE WESTERN WALL WITHOUT BEING THERE So it's come to this. You can sit in your room thousands of miles away from Jerusalem, and with your computer, you can follow the tradition of leaving a prayer or a request in the Western Wall. So long as what you request isn't anti-Semitic or "uncivilized," *aish.com* will place it in the wall for you. You can even send them a small contribution to say thank you right on their site. For that, you don't have to go to Jerusalem.

🖥 www.aish.com/w/p/46889532.html

~ ✡ ~ ✡ ~ ✡ ~

FASTING & FEASTING & YOM KIPPUR

A GUIDE TO FEASTING & FASTING THROUGH THE FIVE MAJOR JEWISH HOLIDAYS New Yorkers know that the way to tell if a Jewish holiday is an important one is if they suspend the alternate side of the street parking rules. But here's a universal way to tell which Jewish holiday it is by what you eat (or don't eat) during it. *Oy Vey: More* is one of many places where you'll find this famous satirical look at the holidays.

Rosh Hashanah.............	Feast
Tzom Gedaliah...........	Fast
Yom Kippur...............	More fasting
Sukkot........................	Feast for a week
Hoshanah Rabbah............	More feasting
Simchat Torah.................	Keep right on feasting
Month of Cheshvan..........	No feasts or fasts for a whole month. Get a grip on yourself.
Hanukkah........................	Eat potato pancakes
Tenth of Tevet.................	Do not eat potato pancakes

Tu B'Shevat	Feast
Fast of Esther................	Fast
Purim............................	Eat pastry
Passover........................	Do not eat pastry for a week
Shavuot.........................	Dairy feast (cheesecake, blintzes, etc.)
17th of Tammuz.............	Fast (definitely no cheesecake or blintzes)
Tisha B'Av.....................	Serious fast (don't even think about cheesecake or blintzes)
Month of Elul.................	End of cycle. Enroll in Center for Eating Disorders before High Holidays arrive again.

WHY SOME JEWS BUY SUPPOSITORIES FOR YOM KIPPUR Buck Wolf, who can be counted on to dig up great stories for the weird section of *HuffingtonPost.com,* shared that in some religious communities, there's a run on caffeine suppositories right before Yom Kippur.

While many of people's stomachs can get through the day without eating, their heads need the caffeine jolt their coffee provides. Caffeine also suppresses the hunger drive for many, which helps during the fast. And these suppositories are easy to purchase over the counter or online. Some Orthodox Jews take caffeine suppositories at sundown before the fast, and or/during it. Then they can concentrate better on atoning.

But do they need to atone for *the suppositories?* Perhaps. "We're supposed to do it the old fashioned way—I wouldn't advise [suppositories]," said **Rabbi Simcha Weinstein,** a Hasidic leader. "We want to keep Jews in the synagogue and not in the bathroom."

But one person who took it over Yom Kippur told *The Brooklyn Paper* that throughout the day "I had so much energy, I could have built a Third Temple."

HOW A SHOFAR CAN TELL WHAT TIME IT IS

Cousin Irving was staying over at cousin Shmul's house and woke up in the middle of the night.

Soon Irving was up too. "What time is it?" asked Shmul.

"I don't know," said Shmul. "But I've got a shofar and it will tell me the time."

"How will it do that?" asked Irving.

"I'll open the window and blow it and soon people will be shouting. 'Stop that noise. Do you realize it's __ o'clock in the morning.'"

STUDY SHOWS FASTING DURING YOM KIPPUR CAN CAUSE HEADACHES Like we needed a study to tell us that? It's called the "The Yom Kippur headache" and also the "first of Ramadan headache" since Moslems also fast. And the cure is ... aspirin. Like we needed a study for that too? But yes, they did do a study and found that almost half of those who abstain from food and water all day for their fast get headaches. Presumably, it's caused by dehydration or caffeine withdrawal for coffee nuts deprived of their daily fix.

One thing you may not know: *Reuters* revealed that Israeli researchers found that if you took the drug etoricoxib before the fast, you wouldn't get that headache any time during the day. Sounds good—until you look at the side effects. You might prefer the headache.

THE MAN WHO WAS DESPERATE DURING YOM KIPPUR

A man went up to the rabbi during the break in the Yom Kippur services and pleaded to let him have a glass of water.

"It's not allowed," said the rabbi.

"But I'm desperate," the man replied. "You're allowed to have water if it's a matter of life and death."

Reluctantly, the rabbi agreed. "Oh thank you," said the man after drinking the water. "That's the last time I'll have salted herring for breakfast on Yom Kippur."

RELIGIOSITY (LIGHT)

HILARIOUS WAYS CHILDREN DESCRIBE THE BIBLE

These were submitted to the discussion groups for *all-creatures.org* and have gone around the internet as "The Children's Bible in a Nutshell."

The Bible says, "The Lord thy God is one," but I think He must be a lot older than that.

Adam and **Eve** disobeyed God by eating one bad apple, so they were driven from the Garden of Eden. Not sure what they were driven in though because they didn't have cars.

Noah built a large boat and put his family and some animals on it. He asked some other people to join him, but they said they would have to take a rain check.

Moses real name was **Charlton Heston.**

The [ten] plagues included frogs, mice, lice, bowels, and no cable.

One of Moses' best helpers was **Joshua**. [He] fought the battle of Geritol and the fence fell over on the town.

After Joshua came **David**. He had a son named **Solomon** who had about 300 wives and 500 porcupines. My teacher says he was wise, but that doesn't sound very wise to me.

Jesus had many arguments with sinners like the Pharisees and the Republicans. Jesus also had twelve opossums. The worst one was Judas Asparagus. Judas was so evil that they named a terrible vegetable after him.

BEING NAMED GOD MAY NOT BE A BLESSING Have things gotten so bad that even God couldn't get a loan? It looked that way, except that it wasn't our God (Yahweh), but a man named God, namely **God Gazarov**. That really is his name, and he's a Russian Jew, named after his grandfather.

According to a lawsuit he filed in Brooklyn, the major credit agency, Equifax, refused to accept that God was actually his legitimate first name. In frustration, he said that he never claimed that he was "the almighty leader of the world." It didn't matter; apparently, even an act of God couldn't help him.

God, this one, found that he couldn't get a car dealer to loan him money, even though he had impeccable credit. And Equifax's impious suggestion was that he should change his name. The other two agencies, TransUnion, and Experian, were obviously more reverent than Equifax and rated him over 720. After five years of struggle, and a lot of publicity, he finally was allowed to "keep" his name.

Take heart, if you've ever had trouble with a credit agency. You are not alone. For years, not even God could get those guys to see the light.

THE MAN WHO SOLD HIS AFTERLIFE Timeshares are usually a rip-off, but one Jewish man tried to sell the ultimate real estate on eBay: eternity in Heaven. The bidding started at $0.99 but soon hit $100,000, showing a limitless willingness to bid on a piece of blue sky.

The seller, **Ari Mandel**, pointed out that he has none of the sins that would permanently keep him out of Heaven, even though he's now a vegan atheist. Even those he claimed to be selling points: being vegan, he eats no *treif*, and being an atheist, worships no false idols. He also promised that if he did something crazy, like becoming a Born Again, he would compensate the buyer for the fair market value of his little slice of Heaven.

Naturally, eBay canceled the auction, and Mandel said he was joking, and so perhaps was the $100,000 bidder. Another one who may have been having a bit of a giggle, or perhaps was just a hard bargainer, was the man who was skeptical of the location of the real estate. "For the price you are asking, I want to make sure I am in prime real estate, somewhere over a rainbow, right between the Lord and a few angels." After all, it wouldn't do to overpay to end up in a tacky part of heaven.

YES, YOU CAN BREAK THE SABBATH RULES Sabbath rules are suspended if a person's life is in danger. So, as *Judaism for Dummies* says: "Hypothetically, if you have a terrible life-threatening disease, and the only cure is to cook (which is prohibited on Sabbath) and eat pork (which you're never allowed), you've got to do it."

BUT BURY PEOPLE QUICKLY

When someone dies, in the Jewish tradition, they must be buried quickly. **Billy Crystal**, in the wonderful show *700 Sundays* said: "I had an uncle who was narcoleptic, and he would nod off, and immediately you heard digging."

WHY JEWS FOR JESUS IS NOT A KOSHER GROUP This cult, whose real purpose is to convert Jews, led **comedian Jackie Mason** to say of them: There's no such thing as a Jew for Jesus. It's like saying a black man is for the KKK.

RELIGIOSITY (SERIOUS)

WHAT IS CHABAD—AND WHAT IS A MITZVAH TANK?
People call it a "Mitzvah Tank," but this mini synagogue on wheels (sometimes jokingly referred to in New York as a "Mikvahmobile") is an RV van that travels to major cities where there are Jews, or people who might want to become Jewish.

Chabad or Lubavitch is now the largest Jewish organization in the world. There may be more Chabad Centers than Starbucks except in South Dakota. But occasionally their "Roving Rabbis" pay a visit. Chabad is also in about 80 countries, including Congo and Cambodia, where there are probably even fewer Jews.

FAMOUS CHABADNIKS Bob Dylan, who was born **Robert Zimmerman,** is probably one of the best-known supporters of Chabad, although he's been known to support a lot of things, including Christianity at one point in his life. But according to a Talmudic blog, *tzvee.blogspot.com,* Dylan was called to the "Torah for an aliyah by his Hebrew name, Zushe ben Avraham."

Over the years, many non-Jews, as well as MOTs (members of the tribe, in other words, Jews) have appeared in the annual Chabad telethons. According to *jewishjournal.com,* they include **Robin Williams, Adam Sandler, James Caan, Martin Sheen, Adam Lambert,** singer (and black-Jewish convert) **Sammy Davis, Jr., Al Gore, Jerry Lewis** and **Bob Saget**.

During one telethon, **Bob Hope,** and **Larry King** kept mispronouncing the name as "Sha-bad." The story quotes the telethon's producer, **Chaim Marcus,** as saying to Larry King, "Larry, it's chhhh—you know, like Chhhaim, Chhhannukah, chhhutzpah, chhhhallah."

People who called in pledges and/or helped the shows have included **Frank Sinatra, Marlon Brando, Barbra Streisand, John Denver, Van Halen's David Lee Roth,** comedian **Richard Lewis, Sammy Davis Jr., Carroll O'Connor** and **Jon Voigt.**

GUIDE FOR THE GOYIM

WHAT YOU SHOULD KNOW ABOUT SOME JEWISH WORDS AND EXPRESSIONS

WHAT DOES "WHAT AM I, CHOPPED LIVER?" MEAN? Have you ever had a Jewish meal where chopped liver was the main course? No, it's the side dish. When someone asks, "What am I, chopped liver?" they feel they're being ignored or shunted aside.

WHAT DOES IT MEAN TO MAKE A "BIG TZIMMES" OVER SOMETHING? The expression comes from the Jewish food dish tzimmes, which requires a lot of cutting and slicing. So, to make a big tzimmes over something means to make a big deal over it, usually in a situation where it's inappropriate."Don't make such a big tzimmes over this. It's nothing."

WHY ARE NATIVE-BORN ISRAELIS CALLED SABRAS? The name comes from a cactus which is tough on the outside and soft and sweet on the inside, supposedly what Israelis are like.

WHEN DO JEWS SAY SHALOM? Anytime instead of "hello" and "goodbye."

WHAT'S WITH THE GEFILTE FISH? No, Virginia, there is no Gefilte Fish swimming around in the water. Mainly, the "fish" is a mélange of carp, pike, mullet, whitefish, Nile perch, and there's even pink gefilte fish using salmon.

Gefiltephiles please note: There are 12,200 entries for Gefilte Fish on YouTube. A few: *Holy Carp: Gefilta Fish; Judaism and Me; The Gefilte Fish Chronicles* (a DVD, book and musical).

WHY DO JEWS GRIT THEIR TEETH WHEN SOMEONE SAYS TO THEM "SOME OF MY BEST FRIENDS ARE JEWISH"? Would someone say: "Some of my best friends are Catholics"? "Some of my best friends are Italians"? Why emphasize the difference between groups? Many think that even making the "friends" claim (usually as a defense) is construed as *ipso facto* evidence of racism. And don't say or write that he's a

"Jewish gentleman" either. Would you say (or write) that someone is a "Catholic gentleman?"

CAN I CALL SOMEONE A JEW? Because of ancient and modern historical connotations, "Jew" used as a pejorative isn't just the shortening of the name of the religion. It's like calling someone [a racist name]. But it's OK if *we* say it, says writer **Sam Greenspan.**

CAN I CALL SOMEONE A "YID?" It depends on how you pronounce it. If you say it like the word "bead" (Yeed), it just means Jewish. But if when you say it so it rhymes with "hid," it's pejorative.

JOKING JEWISH WORDS

Here are some made-up words that only a Jew would understand, printed in *aish.com's* funny site: *Jewlarious.com*

DIS-KVELLIFIED: To drop out of law school, med school or business school as seen through the eyes of parents, grandparents and Uncle Sid.

MATZILATION: Smashing a piece of matzah to bits while trying to butter it.

MINYASTICS: Going to incredible lengths to find a tenth person to complete a minyan.

OY-STER: Defined in *The Washington Post* as someone who sprinkles his conversation with Jewish words, like "oy."

RE-SHTETLEMENT: Moving from Brooklyn to Boca Raton and finding all your old neighbors live in the same condo building as you.

SHOFARSOGUT: The relief you feel when, after many attempts, the shofar is finally blown at the end of Yom Kippur.

YIDENTIFY: To determine Jewish origins of celebrities, even though their names don't sound Jewish.

CHAPTER 12

NOSHING OR KOSHER FOOD & WINE
FOOD, GLORIOUS FOOD

✡

SABBATH SWEETS! MARIJUANA COOKIES ARE SERVED AT HADASSAH HOSPITAL! The *TimesofIsrael.com* reported that there's a licensed medicinal marijuana provider who sells Passover cookies made with pot—and that a major client is Hadassah Hospital! The story was written by **Mitch Ginsburg**, their military correspondent, a good choice for a writer in case they get blasted for this story.

Where these cookies are baked is like a military secret, except that it's "in the center of the country." But the name of the master pastry chef--and entrepreneur--has been revealed: it's **Moshe Ichiya**.

Moshe Ichiya became highly motivated after seeing cancer patients with only one lung chain-smoking medical marijuana. He wanted to make a smoke-free product, so in addition to cookies, he offers marijuana creams and drops as well. Which is good for his orthodox customers who can use these products over Shabbat.

The company is perfectly named, "Cannabliss"—don't bother looking, it's not on the Internet or Facebook—and it's registered with the Health Ministry to supply these cookies to the Hadassah-Hebrew University Medical Center. But the 350 Hadassah patients (and their doctors) requesting it must undergo a complicated approval process. Besides these patients, though, the article claims there are 9,000 licensed users of "therapeutic marijuana," the highest per capita rate in the world, according to the Knesset Drug

Abuse Committee.

To make the cookies kosher for Passover, Ichiya boils all the pots and makes the cookies from matzo meal or potato flour. Since it's given as medicine, it requires no rabbinic supervision. And like everything else that's vague about his operation, he says, "a Rabbi from Mea Shearim" has given the products his blessing.

People who use these cookies say they are absolutely delicious. But is it OK to use marijuana if you're very religious? Even orthodox stoners, who want a Biblical citation to justify its use, point out that in Genesis 1:29, (depending on the translation) God said: "Behold, I have given you every plant yielding seed that is on the surface of all the earth." And that would include marijuana.

YOU WOULD NEVER HAVE TASTED THESE IF NOT FOR JEWS Egg cream, Tootsie rolls, Sara Lee brownies and Sacher-Torte are just a few of the goodies you never would have known of if not for Jews. Here are a few more.

Haagen-Dazs ice cream was invented by **Reuben Mattus**, supposedly as a tribute to the way Denmark treated its Jews. More likely, it was because it sounded foreign, and Denmark had a positive image for dairy products, unlike the Bronx where he was from.

If you drink orange juice for breakfast, it's probably because of **Albert Lasker**, considered to be the father of modern advertising. At the age of 28, he acquired the Sunkist account, at a time that people viewed oranges as something good to prevent scurvy if you were a gold miner. He not only got people to eat oranges, but popularized drinking it for breakfast. Unfortunately, he also got women to smoke Lucky Strikes by convincing them that smoking would keep them slim, but that is another story.

To help you prepare the above—and everything else—one of the most popular cookbooks ever, *The Joy of Cooking,* which has been in continuous print since 1936, was written by two Jews,

Rombauer and **Becker.**

Finally, to help you get rid of all the food you'll eat from the items above, there's Ex-Lax, a company founded by a 27-year old Jew.

HEIMISHE FOOD LABELS

He'brew, the chosen beer, Maccabeans, Meshuggamints, Meshuga nuts, Shalom, the chosen gum, Oy vay, Fancy Shmancy, a hand sanitizer.

FOOD ITEMS TO BUY

A COFFEE KOSHEROLOGIST TELLS HOW TO EAT (& DRINK) KOSHER AT STARBUCKS The *New York Times* interviewed **Uri Ort,** a "coffee kosherologist," who explained that making items kosher at Starbucks is mostly in how they are washed. "If a tool used for a non-kosher drink is used on say, a latte, it causes big problems."

But *thedailymeal.com* was a bit more specific. They said you can eat Tazo tea and hot chocolate, but you can't drink Frappuccino and white hot chocolate. And caramel drizzle is a no-no, but the mocha drizzle and whipped cream sizzles.

Ort points out for those who are really strict about this should know that their dishwashers only heat up to 180 degrees, which is sanitary, but "hot enough to absorb non-kosher particles into a washed pot."

You can check up on Ort's menu to see what's kosher and what's not.

http://tinyurl.com/olbecok

Or, you can go to their Facebook page and argue about these things:

www.facebook.com/kosherstarbucks

GOT A COLD? HERE ARE THE FIVE BRANDS OF CHICKEN SOUP PROVEN TO BE BETTER THAN GRANDMA'S Chicken soup is not just good for the soul— it's good for a cold too. And what you learned as a child and what Jews have known since the 12th century was recently proven in a scientific study by **Dr. Stephen Rennard**, a pulmonologist at the University of Nebraska Medical Center.

He was quoted by *ABC NEWS* as saying that while chicken soup isn't a "cure for the common cold, the proof is in the pudding that it does indeed provide relief from the symptoms." He tested what some people call "Jewish penicillin" against several brands and a regular hot water broth. He concluded: "Some ingredient in the soup blocks or slows the number of cells congregating in the lung area, possibly relieving the development of these cold symptoms."

To prove this, he used a recipe from his Lithuanian grandmother, but he also tested 13 commercial brands as well. The following canned chicken soups worked even better than the homemade. Knorr Chicken Noodle, Campbell's Home Cookin' Chicken Vegetable, Campbell's Healthy Request Chicken Noodle, Lipton Cup-a-Soup Chicken Noodle, Progresso Chicken Noodle.

"You hate it when your grandma's soup doesn't come in first," Rennard says: "But in our house, in terms of which one tastes best, grandma's soup wins hands down. So next time you have a cold, forget your grandmother and have one of the five chicken soup brands above. "Just because your grandma said something doesn't mean that it's not true," he wrote.

ISRAELI VS AMERICAN BAGELS and where to find them
The bagels you'll find in Israel don't look like the bagels you find in New York, which have been described as "donuts with rigor mortis."

Israeli donuts are larger, thinner, more oblong and smothered in sesame seeds.

Bar Bolonat (611 Hudson Street) is now serving these Jerusalem-style bagels with olive oil and zaatar for dipping, just like in Israel. The New York version is about half the size of its Holy Land counterpart, and at $6, costs more. But it's perfect if you're homesick for Israel. Or on a high-carb diet.

NOTE: If you want more bang for your bagels, go to this YouTube titled "You've been Eating Bagels Wrong All Your Life."

💻http://tinyurl.com/pq9jfox

FOR THE SMELL OF EGG CREAM—GO TO YOUR COMPUTER If you go online, you can buy genuine egg cream candles from Katz's delicatessen in New York. "Transform any room into a delicious blast from the past," they promise. And while you're at the site, you can also buy everything from their matzo ball soup to a Passover dinner for two ($75). Plus a T-shirt that says on the back: "Send a Salami to Your Boy in the Army."

💻www.katzsdelicatessen.com/order

IS IT KOSHER?

WHY DID A GROUP OF RABBIS SHMEAR LOX? *The New York Post* called it a "shmear campaign" when a group of super-Orthodox rabbis said certain fish (salmon, cod, tilapia, flounder, and halibut) were unkosher because they host a tiny parasitic worm called anisakis.

The Post also called it a lox-down.

Grubstreet.com pointed out that most rabbis disagree with this group. Even so, lox of luck getting people to stop eating it.

WATER WATER EVERYWHERE BUT NOT A (KOSHER) DROP TO DRINK New Yorkers have a lot to worry about. Crime. Terrorism. Finding a parking spot. And if they're Jewish, add finding a good deli, and checking when sundown will be on the Sabbath. Among the bright points is that at least they haven't had to worry about their water, which is rated as among the best and healthiest tap water on the planet.

But now the *New York Times* went and spoiled it, giving orthodox Jews a new worry. Is New York water kosher? Perhaps that thought just planted a bug in your brain because it turns out there is a bug in the water. The problem is a Copepod, and if you have good eyesight, and a strong stomach, you can sometimes see these when you're about to drink the water.

These critters are crustaceans, you know...shellfish. (Don't be shellfish! The puns make themselves up.) They're sort of itty bitty shrimp, and if you consume New York tap water, you've probably ingested millions of them.

Some Kosher restaurants announce that their water is filtered, so at least the *frum* [religious] don't have to worry that the bugs are still there. Rabbinical opinions differ on the kashruth status of these tiny creatures. Some view them as a major *traif*; others as too trivial to constitute an affront to the deity. So Jew or not, don't start looking for them before you drink up or you could die of worry—or dehydration. Not to mention leaving a bad taste in your mouth.

THE RABBI WHO ATE PORK

An old Jewish joke starts with the premise that there was a rabbi who was dying to try pork, but didn't dare do it for fear someone in his congregation would see him. So he went to a faraway town and ordered a roast pig at a restaurant.

The waiter brought him a huge pig with the traditional apple stuffed in its mouth. The Rabbi took his knife and fork and was about to dive into the dish when he heard a shocked voice asking, "Rabbi? What are you doing?"

He looked around, and there was Mrs. Goldberg from his shul. Thinking quickly, he said: "I ordered an apple, and this is how they brought it."

THAT'S NOT KOSHER

WHY NON-JEWISH PRISONERS ORDER KOSHER FOOD
Under the headline: "You Don't Have to Be Jewish to Love a Kosher Prison Meal," *The New York Times* wrote that an increasing number of non-Jewish prisoners are ordering kosher meals. Since the cost can be four times a standard one, prison executives are not happy. Republican Florida Senator **Greg Evers** remarked about people who shouldn't legitimately be requesting it but do so. "Is bread and water considered kosher? Just a thought. Just a thought."

There are several reasons why they request them. They may be bartered for other items, like cigarettes, or worse. Some prisoners request special meals because the food is boxed elsewhere, so they don't have to worry about whether sex offenders are handling the food they're served. And doing worse than just handling.

The standard for whether a prisoner is entitled to a kosher meal is generally if they hold a "sincere belief" in Judaism. But what's that? "Attempts by prison officials and rabbis to quiz prisoners about the Torah and the rules of keeping kosher were ruled not kosher," wrote the *Times*.

HOW TO TELL IF A PRISONER'S BELIEF IN JUDAISM IS SINCERE How many prisoners might have a "sincere belief" in Judaism, which would qualify them for a kosher meal? The Aleph Institute says that less than 1.5 percent of the country's 1.9 million inmates are Jewish. And ironically, many of them don't ask for kosher food.

Frank Cerabino, of the *Palm Beach Post*, who's probably the funniest columnist today, suggested a test for inmates to see if they have a "sincere belief" in Judaism. Here are a few of the questions he suggested they might ask the inmates.

"When working in the prison kitchen, it's really important to sneak some supplies back to the cell for barter—or keep the dairy silverware separate from the meat silverware?

"I have a nightmare that a correctional officer forced me to snitch on my celly—or eat a cheeseburger.

"What best describes a reason for you to fast behind bars? Abscessed toothor—everything's traif?

"Most of what I know about eating kosher comes from my Muslim cellmate, **Woody Allen** movies, or *The Book of Leviticus.*"

WINE

DOES KOSHER WINE HAVE TO TASTE SO BAD? Adam Montefiore, considered the dean of Israel's wine industry, told *thedailymeal.com:* "In America, if you put the word 'kosher' on sausages, you'll sell more meat. But it's not true for wine."

One wine that many dislike is "mevushal" wine. That's the only kosher wine that doesn't have to be supervised and can even be served by a non-Jew to an orthodox one. Traditionally, it was boiled, but now it undergoes flash pasteurization. Some think that affects its taste, and that it's rubbery, sweet and tastes like cough syrup. Your grandmother, however, loved it.

WHY IS THIS KOSHER WINE DIFFERENT FROM ALL OTHER WINES? You wouldn't know that some wines were kosher if you didn't read the label. The only difference is it's made under the direction of a rabbi. The wine tasting director at *Wine Enthusiast* magazine, **Lauren Buzzeo,** reminds us that kosher wines can't contain any additives or traif. However, while all ingredients in kosher wine must be kosher-certified, most wine ingredients are already kosher.

The wine-making has to be supervised by a mashgiah (Jew who supervises the Kashruth) In every step, kosher wine can be handled only by Sabbath-observant Jews, including the harvesting of the grapes. And, how many Mexican farm workers can you find who keep the Sabbath?

IS IT KOSHER TO MAKE YOUR OWN (KOSHER) WINE AT HOME? While wine may be kosher, it may not be kosher to the government. The head of a family is allowed to produce only up to 200 gallons of wine for home consumption annually without paying tax. That's a lot of vino—even for a wino. Still, you may have to register with the government before you start making your spirits or they may spirit your money away.

Is that likely to happen? As they said in the *First Jewish Catalog:* "I've never heard of any recent wine busts, however, and in the only case that I know that ever came to court, the judge fined the victim one dollar and asked for his recipe."

WHEN JEWS ARE THIRSTY

The Italian says, "I'm thirsty. I must have wine.

The Russian says, "I'm thirsty. I must have vodka."

The German says, "I'm thirsty. I must have beer."

The Mexican says, "I'm thirsty. I must have tequila."

The Jewish man:, "I'm thirsty. I must have diabetes."

JUST SO YOU SHOULD KNOW

Israeli stamps are certified kosher.

There's a McDonald's at Masada. For this maybe 1000 people died?

Your toothpaste may not be kosher because it usually contains cornstarch. But go ahead and use it—unless you plan to eat it.

There are over 145 Passover cookbooks listed on amazon. A great one is *The New York Times Passover Cookbook* by **Linda Amster.**

CHAPTER 13
YIDDISH & HEBREW

YIDDISH WORDS

YINGLISH: YOU MAY BE SPEAKING YIDDISH WHEN YOU SAY Billy Crystal once described Yiddish as a combination of German and phlegm. "Yinglish" was the word used by **Leo Rosten** in *Joys of Yiddish* to describe these words, and Wikipedia, under "Yiddish Words Used in English" has an entire page listing over 200 of them. Here are a few they listed that even the goyim might use without realizing they're speaking Yiddish.

CHUTZPAH: audacity, nerve...**DRECK:** rubbish, trash... **GLITCH:** a minor malfunction (possibly from Yiddish glitsh)...**GOY:** someone not of the Jewish faith or people...**KIBITZ**: to converse idly, gossip, chat...**KITSCH:** gaudy trash...**KLUTZ:** clumsy person... **KOSHER:** conforming to Jewish dietary laws...**KVETCH:** to complain habitually...**MAVEN:** trusted expert...**MENSCH:** a decent human being...**NEBBISH:** a hapless, unfortunate person...**NOSH:** snack...**OY:** Oh!...**SCHLEMIEL:** aninept clumsy person...**SCHLEP:** to drag or haul (an object)... **SCHLOCK:** A poorly made product or poorly done work... **SCHMOOZE:** to converse informally...**SHIKSA:** a Gentile woman...**SHPIEL:** a lengthy talk...**CHOTCHKE:** knick-knack, trinket...**TSURIS:** troubles...**TUSH:** backside... **Leo Rosten** in *The Joy of Yiddish* added a few, saying you're speaking Yiddish if you say **AHA, AMEN, LOX, SHLEP, TUCHIS.**

YIDDISH WORDS YOU CAN USE IN SCRABBLE More than 300 Yiddish and Hebrew words are all officially acceptable in Scrabble. Here are a few of the best-known ones: **SCHMUTZ, TUCHIS, MITZVAH, ALIYAH, TALLIS, SHLUB, and SHLEP.**

What is the most used word? **Nosh.**

Finally, you can't say "goy" but you can say "shiksa." Is that a shonda? Sorry, can't say that word either.

WHAT A SHLIMAZEL Those of you who remember the old TV sitcom *Laverne & Shirley* may recall the word "Shlimazel," a Yiddish-American chant that opened each show. In 1984, the word "shlimazel" was one of the ten non-English words that a British translation company claimed was the hardest to translate. Not according to *UrbanDictionary.com*, which defines it as someone with constant bad luck. "When the shlemiel spills his soup, he probably spills it on the schlimazel," they wrote.

FROM THE JEWISH COMMITTEE TO PRESERVE THE ENGLISH LANGUAGE

The author of this is unknown, but it was quoted in *Oy Vey: More.*

"To all the schlemiels, nebbishes, nudniks, klutzes, putzes, shlubs, shmoes, shmucks, and no-goodniks out there, I get sentimental when I think about English and its important place in our society. Oy! I'm ready to plotz when I hear these mavens kvetching about our national language being bastardized. What chutzpah! These nebbishes can spiel about the cultural and linguistic diversity of our country and of English itself being lost to shlock, but I'm not buying their fershlugganah shtick. It's all a bunch of dreck. We have English and they have bubkes. People who think there are too many foreign words in English are just a big pain in the tuchis."

A BISSEL WEIRD

YIDDISH EVERY JEWISH DOG SHOULD KNOW Marjorie Gottlieb Wolfe, in her funny book, *Yiddish for Dog & Cat Lovers*, listed a few dog obedience commands for those who want their dogs to be bilingual. You can probably try these on your cat, but he/she probably isn't going to obey you in any language anyway. ZITZ, KUM, GEFIN, (find) GUT, HEY OYF.

And finally, there's the phrase every dog should know: "Don't eat that, it's not kosher." *"Du zalst nit esn az es s nit kosher."*

OFFFBEAT YIDDISH BOOK TITLES *Born to Kvetch; Dirty Yiddish; Drek: The Real Yiddish Your Bubbe Never Taught You; Yiddish with Dick & Jane; Complete Idiot's Guide to Learning Yiddish; Yiddish for Babies.* (For example, they translated in Yiddish, "Baby loves her grandpa even though he's an 'alter kocker'.")*Yiddish Yoga; Yiddish Rhyming Dictionary; The Shiksa's Guide To Yiddish; If You Can't Say Anything Nice, Say It In Yiddish.*

HOW YIDDISH COULD LEAD TO WORLD PEACE The Yiddish poet **Moishe Leib Halpern** said that all declarations of war should be issued in Yiddish. That would effectively guarantee peace in the world because almost no one could read it.

HEBREW VS. YIDDISH

A fun book titled *Are Yentas, Kibitzers & Tummlers Weapons of Mass Instruction? Yiddish Trivia* by **Marjorie** Gottlieb Wolfe, relates the old story of a mother in Israel on a bus talking to her son in Yiddish while the child kept talking Hebrew.

"Speak Yiddish," the mother admonished him.

A man nearby said ""Excuse me lady, but why do you insist that your son speak Yiddish?"

"I don't want he should forget that he's Jewish," she said.

SO NU?

THREE UNEXPECTED NON-JEWISH STARS WHO SPOKE YIDDISH Jews aren't that surprised when a Jew speaks Yiddish in a movie, although non-Jews may think they're talking gibberish! For example, the chief in the **Mel Brooks** movie *Blazing Saddles*. But non-Jews speaking a *bissel* Yiddish?

Robin Williams spoke Yiddish so well that he told the *Jewishjournal.com*, "People tend to think I'm Jewish." He said it was a great language for comedy, and he thought the greatest word of all was "nu," because it encompasses everything. "What? How are you? Everything good? Bad?"

Tough guy **James Cagney**, who won an Oscar for playing **George M. Cohan** in *Yankee Doodle Dandy,* spoke Yiddish in a few of his films, including *Taxi* and *The Fighting 69th*. According to *JewishHumorCentral.com,* (a hilarious website) the Irish/Norwegian actor learned Yiddish when he was growing up in New York's East Side.

Add Yiddish to the languages spoken by **Marlon Brando,**who also spoke French, Spanish, Japanese, Italian and German. Brando learned Yiddish from his acting teacher, **Stella Adler**, whose daughter he dated. But according to the *jewishjournal.com,* Stella's family of famed Yiddish actors disapproved of the match because he wasn't Jewish. Their attitude may have been summed up by Brando's words in *Apocalypse Now*, "The Horror."

COLLEGES IN AMERICA THAT TEACH YIDDISH David **Steinberg** once said: "My father never lived to see his dream come true of an all-Yiddish-speaking Canada." OK, he was kidding. But if you think Yiddish is dead, *yiddishbookcenter.org,* an interesting website, listed over 20 colleges and universities that teach Yiddish.

Robert Alper, a Rabbis and stand-up comedian, says that in his university, Hebrew, Russian and German languages are all in the same building. "We call it the Department of Semitic and Anti-Semitic Languages," he joked.

HEBREW

BET YOU DIDN'T KNOW YOU COULD BE SPEAKING HEBREW WHEN YOU SAID THESE WORDS According to *cooljew.com,* these words have a Hebrew derivation.

ABRACADABRA   (literal Hebrew translation "I create what I speak").

ALPHABET
AMEN
CAMEL
HALLELUJAH
JEW
JOE SHMO
JUBILEE
KOSHER
MESSIAH
RABBI
SABBATH,
ZION.

FOUR FUNNY HEBREW SLOGANS ON T-SHIRTS

YOU HAD ME AT SHALOM;
HEBREW SCHOOL DROPOUT;
SHALOM Y'ALL;
CHAI MAINTENANCE
[Available at *CafePress.com* and *Israeli-t.com*]

CHAPTER 14
LIFE IN ISRAEL

DAILY LIFE

IT'S MUCH SAFER IN ISRAEL THAN AMERICA We frequently hear news from Israel about some terrorist attack or its aftermath, making people believe that everyone who leaves their home, or the King David Hotel, or from wherever, is unlikely to get very far before being violently dispatched.

Unsurprisingly, dramatic and violent events involving terrorism over there attract a lot of media attention. But most of the violent crimes and murders in America are pretty much ignored as routine. Here, the only major attention given is to mass shootings. So that people are lulled into thinking that unless they're someplace like a mall, a school, or a post office, they're likely to be safe. Pretty much unreported in the United States, though, are all kinds of common violence: robberies gone wrong, street crime, domestic murders, and myriad other ways to get killed.

But Israel has strong security. And strong gun control laws. In the wake of previous attacks and attempts, they've been forced to secure schools, theaters, malls and other places with security guards. Indeed, the very places in the U.S. favored by our own homegrown crazies.

It, therefore, shouldn't be surprising that the actual murder rate in the United States, 4.7 per 100,000 (Wikipedia), is more than twice that of Israel's. So, if you haven't traveled to Israel for fear of the "violence," instead, think twice when you venture out right in the "good" ole USA. And go to Israel—you'll be safer there.

SIXTEEN THINGS THAT ONLY HAPPEN IN ISRAEL
Ephraim Kishon was a Jewish humorist who came to Israel in 1949 and died in 2005. Here's what he noticed in his later years about his adopted country.

It is the only country where on Fridays when you go to your parents, everyone sits exactly where he sat at the age of five.

It is the only country where the unemployed strike.

It is a country surrounded on all sides by enemies, but the people's headaches are caused by the neighbors upstairs.

Israel is the only country in the world where "small talk" consists of loud, angry debate over politics and religion.

It is the only country where there is no problem to find software for launching satellites, but you have to wait a week to fix your washing machine.

It is the only country that has a communications satellite, but no one lets you finish a sentence.

It is the only country where no woman gets along with her mother, but still talks to her three times a day, two of them about you.

This is the only country where the corporal's mother has the commander's phone and he should be warned.

It is the only country where football players bring their dads to shout at the coach.

Natan Gesher, an Israeli citizen who lived in Israel for seven years, posted to *Quora.com* that...

Only in Israel can you tell your boss that he's an idiot and he's running the company into the ground, and still have a job the next day.

Only in Israel can you go to a wedding in blue jeans and sandals.

Only in Israel can you know what the security situation is by the songs on the radio.

Benji Lovitt, blogging in the *TimesofIsrael.com*, gave another reason he loves Israel: I love how the doors to apartment buildings are left open or unlocked on Shabbat for easy access. Of course, it's safe, the criminals are at dinner too.

FOUR REASONS JOAN RIVERS LOVED ISRAEL

In her book, Drop Dead Diva, Joan Rivers gave a few joking reasons why she loved Israel:

"I love its blue and white flag. It matches my legs.

"I love that Israel reminds me of Boca Raton—palm trees, white sand, and old Jews.

"I love that the Dead Sea was named for my sex life.

"I love that it's not Egypt."

JUST SO YOU SHOULD KNOW

Christians in Israel Israel may be the only safe place for Christians in the Middle East right now. It is also the only place in the Middle East where Christianity is growing and flourishing. Of the 3 & 1/2 million tourists to Israel in 2013, according to the *TimesofIsrael.com,* more than half were Christians, and half of them were Catholic.

Arabs in Israel have more freedom and rights than Arabs anywhere in the Middle East.

TRANSPORTATION & TRAVEL

A FEW WORDS ON ISRAELI TAXI DRIVERS

Comedian **George Burns** once said: "It's too bad all the people who know how to run the country are busy driving taxicabs." Apparently, Israel has the same problem --except some of them there really do know it all. Here is what comedian **Ephraim Koshon** said.

Israel is the only country in the world with bus drivers and taxi drivers who read **Spinoza** and **Maimonides.**

It is the only country where the man with the open shirt and the stain is an honorable minister and the guy next to him with a suit and tie is his driver.

Only in Israel can you be invited to a family dinner by a taxi driver so you can meet his single daughter.

THE FIRST ROLLS-ROYCE IN ISRAEL It took five months of bureaucratic hurdles for the first late model Rolls-Royce Phantom to arrive in Israel, which it did in March of 2014 according to the *algemeiner.com.* The car is owned by one of Israel's leading contractors, who crowed that: "My Ferrari blinded their right eye and the Rolls-Royce will gouge their left." Unassuming he is not.

Apparently, he didn't mind paying almost a quarter of a million dollars for it—and 2/3 of that for the import tariff—for this gem with a 6.6-liter engine and 570 horsepower. Plus leather upholstery (for that money you didn't expect Naugahyde did you?) a mahogany finish, and even an umbrella holder.

Unfortunately for him, when the car needs a regular checkup or repair if anything goes wrong, he has to fly in a team of mechanics to perform basic maintenance. He probably doesn't care. It's like the old joke that if you have to ask what a yacht will cost you, you can't afford it.

Here's a video in Hebrew of him kvelling (bursting with pride): http://tinyurl.com/panvfxm

UNUSUAL PLACES & PEOPLE

THE ELVIS INN IN ISRAEL...WHY? WHY NOT? It's not the Heartbreak Hotel, and it's not at the end of Lonely Street, but in between Tel Aviv and Jerusalem is the small town named Abu Ghosh—whose other claim to notoriety is as the home of the world's largest plate of hummus. And there you'll also find a hotel that's a shrine to the King.

Considering the location, you might think it would be **King David** or some other ancient King with a polysyllabic Biblical name. But the 16-foot gold-colored statue outside of **Elvis Presley** is obviously "the King," although it doesn't really look much like him without his sequins.

The Sistine Chapel-style ceiling inside featuring scenes of Presley's life does not include his Jewish ancestry. Even without it, this shrine is described by Fodor's as: "The largest collection of Elvis memorabilia this side of Graceland."

The guide also notes that it's "probably the only Elvis souvenir shop in the world where you can get shawarma." Elvis's famous peanut butter, bacon and banana on challah sandwich might have been more appropriate.

Haaretz.com notes that: "the prices are mid-range, but the experience is priceless...for that chance to ask yourself why on Earth there is a paean to the Pelvis in the middle of the Judean Hills."

ON THE DARK SIDE: A RESTAURANT WHERE YOU EAT WITHOUT LIGHTS   They say love is blind, but at this restaurant, so are the waiters. And you're eating "blind" because you dine in a pitch black room and can't see the (kosher) food...or anything else there. And if that seems odd, well, so is this place. It's in Jaffa, and it's called the Blackout Restaurant.

The sightless wait staff ushers in the guests, in pitch blackness, like a conga line. Once seated, you can take your chances on the prix fixe dinner. Or you can *really* take your chances and order a "mystery" meal. Not only won't you know what they'll bring you, but you'll have the fun of trying to figure out what it is that you're eating when it arrives. And go ahead and eat some of the food with your fingers— who's going to know? And as if all that wasn't weird enough, afterward you can go to a dimly lit room for coffee—where the waiters are *deaf.*

It's quite an experience, not limited to Israel since there's also blind wait staff restaurants in Switzerland, Germany, Hong Kong, California, Paris, London, and other cities. There's even one in New York, but they just wear blindfolds, which seems like cheating. And don't think *you* can cheat in the dining room by sneaking a look at your cell phone or using its flashlight. They make you leave your phone outside. But if you keep another one in your pocket, who's to know?

A HOTEL FOR ORCHIDS: Orchids aren't like marijuana plants where if you leave them alone, they'll grow and make you money (or happy). No, these very delicate flowers must be nurtured and cared for or you'll end up de-flowered.

That's why an entrepreneur with a way with orchids started "Wendy Nursery" in Modi'in. They do house calls, and they have a "Flower Clinic" to treat dying orchids. They also "plant sit," and promise each plant gets full personal attention since they only "sit" 10 orchids at a time. Reported *nocamels.com,* a site that covers Israeli innovations, they charge about 60 cents per night— "including breakfast and dessert...A full pension." So far, no complaints from the "residents."

SNAKES ALIVE! UNFORTUNATELY, THEY ARE There's a place in Israel where you're more likely to find a person with a snake on someone's back than a person who's a snake in the grass. Although maybe you'll find both.

An Israeli masseuse swears that slithering snakes are therapeutic— and she offers snake massages for those brave enough to want it. Her snakes crawl willy-nilly all over the person who's lying on their stomach—surely too petrified to turn around—because supposedly the slow undulation of the snakes massages the back.

Ada Barak, whose Carnivorous Plant Farm is near Haifa, has invented this snake massage. It involves placing five snakes on the victim's, er, patient's back and letting them loose. "The largest will be eight feet long, a king snake, and good for soothing stiff muscles," she promises. Unconvincingly.

She says she discovered the method when she was delivering a talk on plants. (Who knows what she does with *them*.) A woman in the audience who had recently injured herself in an equestrian accident slithered over to Ada afterward...well, you can just imagine how weird that conversation was.

Not everyone thrills to the idea of being buried under a mass of scaly flesh as a form of therapy. But the 60-year old Barak says: "People fly in from all parts of the world to find my little farm in Israel...as long as people want a snake massage, I shall continue." As they said in *Indiana Jones*, "Snakes. Why did it have to be snakes?"

AMERICANS IN (AND FOR) ISRAEL
SURPRISING SUPPORTERS

SOME SUPERSTARS WHO HAVE VISITED THE WESTERN WALL Michael Douglas sustained what was euphemistically called a "hora-related injury" to his groin at his son's Bar Mitzvah, leaving Michael limping. **Stephanie Butnick** of the *Tabletmag.com* joked, "The hora can be dangerous. There are elderly relatives to watch out for, gnashing stiletto spikes to avoid, plus everyone's going at a completely different speed—and don't get me started about going up those chairs."

Even so, after the Bar Mitzvah, he limped into Israel with his wife, **Catherine Zeta-Jones,** and their son, as part of the celebration at the Western Wall. He also told the world what they had done by making a nice video. That's nice.

💻 www.tabletmag.com/scroll/177606/michael-douglas-says-shalom-from-Israel

Others who have visited the wall, or, as the joke goes, felt like talking to a wall, included **Lady Gaga** (American pop singer and songwriter), **Vladimir Putin (**Russian President), **Madonna** (not the real one; the American pop icon), **President Barack Obama, Pamela Anderson, Mitt Romney, Red Hot Chili Peppers, Sarah Palin, Blair Underwood, Mariah Carey** (depicted wiping away tears at the Wall), **Pope Benedict XVI.**

💻 *TLVFaces.com* printed some photos of celebrities at the Western Wall, and also a video of them there. www.youtube.com/watch?v=3z1A3e1sdto

THREE NON-JEWS WHO SAID SHALOM TO ISRAEL Hillary Clinton kind of spoke out for Israel when it was protecting itself from the Hamas rockets during "Operation Protective Edge" in 2014. "I don't know a nation...that hasn't made errors, but ultimately the responsibility rests with Hamas," *jta.org* quoted her as saying.

She also criticized the "enormous international reaction" against Israel, calling it "uncalled for and unfair," especially "in comparison to the relatively more tepid responses to the far greater death toll in Syria and Russian aggression against Ukraine."

Sharon Stone Although she's not Jewish, she's been married to two Jewish men and was once quoted as saying: "I feel so neurotic that I know what it must feel like to be Jewish." Well, duh, no thank you. Perhaps it's time for you to stop watching all those **Woody Allen** movies.

WELL-KNOWN NON-JEWS WHO HAVE INVESTED HEAVILY IN ISRAELI STARTUPS Serena Williams, tennis player; **Tobey Maguire; Lance Armstrong** (investor in Mobi, an Instagram competitor.) The three of them contributed 6.5 million dollars, revealed *NoCamels.com.* Others include **Leonardo DiCaprio; Jay-Z; Justin Bieber** (invested in 12 startups to date); **Ashton Kutscher** (invested and hosted events for Israeli startups); **Ellen DeGeneres** (did a giveaway of SodaStream); **Michael J. Fox** (over 1 million in grants to two Israeli companies studying Parkinson's).

YOU WOULDN'T HAVE EXPECTED TO SEE THESE PEOPLE IN ISRAEL VIDEOS & COMMERCIALS

Robert Kennedy, in a yarmulka, in Israel in 1948

www.jewsnews.co.il/2013/06/10/robert-kennedys-1948-reports-from-the-holy-land

Robert De Niro once said: "Let me just make sure you got that picture of me in Israel in front of that big Israeli flag to show those anti-Israel d---bags that they are lying sacks of manure."

www.israellycool.com/wordpress/wp-content/uploads/DE-niro-in-Israel-cleaned1.jpg

"Tony Soprano," aka the late **James Gandolfini,** here in a funny commercial for Israel YES satellite channels.

www.jewsnews.co.il/2013/06/28/tony-soprano-in-a-new-funny-advertisement

ENTERTAINERS WHO HAVE STOOD UP FOR ISRAEL

THEY BRAVED THE BOYCOTT TO PLAY IN ISRAEL Alicia Keys, Rihanna, Bee Gees, Tom Jones, Julio Iglesias, Hugh Laurie ("Dr. House" is also a musician), **Paul McCartney** ("I got death threats, but I'm coming anyway," he said), **Elton John, Madonna, Lady Gaga, Justin Bieber, Miley Cyrus,** and **Neil Young**.

DID HE REALLY MARRY HER? Justin Timberlake more than wowed them with music at his Israeli concert. A woman held up a sign saying that her boyfriend had pledged to propose marriage to her if he would take a selfie with the two of them. *Israelycool.com* reported that Timberlake jumped off the stage, took the selfie and said to the groom, "All right. DO IT." The guy was ready with a ring, got down on his knees and to thunderous applause from the crowd, proposed.

🖥 www.youtube.com/watch?v=kOUwkHsnJ9s

Such a great story. The only problem is that it came out later that the "fiancé" had scammed Justin, and the couple was already married.

THE ROLLING STONES GAVE GREAT SATISFACTION The Rolling Stones started their concert in Israel off right—by starting it late. They held it up for an hour so orthodox Jews could drive to it after sunset when Shavuot ended. Ya think they checked a

Jewish calendar? (More likely they checked with a Jewish manager.)

They also satisfied their Israeli fans by using 12 Hebrew phrases during the concert. In one, they introduced themselves by literally translating "rolling stone:""Anachnu HaAvarim Hamitgalgalot."

Alas, *TheJewishIndependent.com* pointed out that: "**Jagger** failed to correctly pronounce the Hebrew letter 'Chet,' which can be enunciated correctly only if you clear your throat at the same time." Who cared, when after the concert, they tweeted a thank you to their fans—in Hebrew.

AWARD WINNERS

TIE A BLUE RIBBON FOR TONY ORLANDO Tony Orlando, who, with **Dawn,** popularized the song "Tie a Yellow Ribbon Round the Ole Oak Tree," visited with the families of three missing hitchhiking Israeli teens when he was in Israel. He also encouraged people to tie a yellow ribbon for them.

SEAN PENN—A SURPRISING HUMANITARIAN Sean Penn, whose father is Jewish and mother Catholic, helped an imprisoned American Orthodox Jew get released from a squalid Bolivian jail on trumped up charges. For this, Penn was given a "Champion of Jewish Values Award" by the Values Network.

BUT DON'T GIVE A "JEWISH" AWARD TO TOM CRUISE OR MICHAEL DOUGLAS...Whoops, too late. Can you believe that a major Jewish organization held a $1,000 a plate dinner to give an award to **Tom Cruise,** a loon who has done enormous damage to Judaism by representing the Scientology cult? Scientology has lured away tens of thousands of people from their Jewish religion, and taken tens of millions of dollars from them that could have gone to good Jewish causes.

As if that wasn't bad enough, in 2014, the million dollar Genesis Prize, sometimes called the Jewish Nobel Prize, was awarded to someone who wasn't even brought up Jewish by his non-Jewish mother, although his father, **Kirk Douglas**, is a famous Jew. **Michael Douglas** also married a non-Jew, **Catherine Zeta-Jones,** and admitted he sometimes felt "alienated from Judaism," since many Jews "don't consider him or his children Jewish." He says he plans to donate the million to some worthy cause. Stay tuned.

ATHEISTS & HALF JEWS WHO HAVE STOOD UP FOR ISRAEL

Uber-atheist**, Bill Maher,** who's half-Jewish and half-Catholic, tweeted during "Operation Protective Edge" that "Dealing w/Hamas is like dealing w/a crazy woman who's trying to kill u—u can only hold her wrists so long before you have to slap her."

Another time he said: "Israel... isn't perfect but it's held to a standard I don't think anybody in the world is expected to live up to.... The idea [of] casting Israel in the role of the oppressor?...what would America do if somebody was lobbing rockets from Toronto? We'd f------ nuke 'em. We're ready to nuke Crimea, and we don't even give a s--- about it! People don't even know where it is! It's insane."

Jay Leno "I'm a huge supporter of Israel and always have been. It is a democracy in the Middle East, and I don't like to see the little guy getting picked on by the big guy."

Scarlett Johansson is being called "a star of David" because, frankly, Scarlet does give a you-know-what. And Scarlett's not yellow when it comes to standing up for Israel. SodaStream, a popular Israel-based "make your own soda at home" firm, has plants in Israel that employ Arabs and pays them the same wages as the Jews. But that didn't stop the boycotters who tried to stop her from being their "first global brand ambassador."

But this superstar, whose mother is Jewish and who describes herself as Jewish, and celebrates Christmas and Hanukkah, said she loves the brand and has used it for years, and that SodaStream's "commitment to a healthier body and a healthier planet is a perfect fit for me."

PETS: DOGS

TELEVISION IS GOING TO THE DOGS (THANKS TO A CAT) Just because you may have to go off to work and can't stay home all day and watch TV doesn't mean your dog can't. When Israeli **Ron Levi** noticed that his cat, Charlie, was obviously enthralled by a custom DVD Levi made for him of birds and fish, Levi thought dogs could use something interesting to watch, too. He also felt that dogs needed "relaxation and stimulation" while their owner was away, even though most dogs would probably prefer to stay home and do nothing but lick their...feet.

Dog TV is currently available—Israel-based Discovery Communications recently purchased a stake in it--in a subscription-only format for $5 a month. Alternatively, you can subscribe to their Internet streaming service directly through DOGTV for $10 a month. (www.dogtv.com)

A NO-BRAINER: ISRAELI-AMERICAN PROJECT WILL TELL YOU WHAT'S ON YOUR DOG'S MIND. (PROBABLY FOOD.) Sure, you think your dog talks to you in his or her own way. But some people think the day will come when we can completely understand every "woof" they say. While this may sound barking mad to some, there's a joint Israeli-American program underway to read the minds of dogs and translate them into human language.

The idea is that when a dog's nose knows something, for example, it detects drugs, a distinctive brainwave pattern is generated. This can be picked up using electronics, like an MRI. These patterns can be stored in a database and recognized when they occur. For instance, the dog's brainwaves could point out a suspect carrying drugs in the street.

Could this lead to a dog (say a legal beagle?) coming to court and "testifying" against someone?

PROSECUTOR: And, Mr. Fido, could you point out the defendant in the audience?

FIDO: Arf! Arf! Arf! Arf!

PROSECUTOR: Let the record reflect that Mr. Fido has identified the defendant...

Some think it will never happen, though others are doggedly determined to make it work. But **Dr. Orit Chai** of the faculty at Koret School of Veterinary Science thinks those working on it are barking up the wrong tree. "It's a long way off to interpret [waves] and transform them into human language. It...sounds like it verges on the bizarre."

SOME DOG BREEDS CAN'T MAKE ALIYAH Want to bring your dog to Israel? If he or she is a Pit Bull Terrier, American Staffordshire Terrier (Amstaff), Bull Terrier, Fila Brazileiro, Staffordshire Bull Terrier (English Staff), Tosa Inu (JapaneseTosa), Rottweiler or Dogo Argentino—or even a cross with those breeds, or writes *nbn.org,* "exhibits behavioral patterns and/or physical traits similar to those of a dangerous breed," you can just leave them home, thank you.

DOG DROPPINGS

JERUSALEM WANTS TO USE DNA ON DOG POOP—AND BUSINESS IS PICKING UP The Jerusalem municipality decided to launch a pilot program to see if they could stop suburban sociopaths from letting their precious puppies befoul the public thoroughfares. The problem: how to tell which dog had left something behind and which owner was the culprit who didn't pick it up afterward?

Enter DNA evidence. Can you see it now? Someone forgets to pick up after their pup. Within minutes, cars converge on the neighborhood, sirens blaring, and an agent draws a chalk outline around the offending ordure. Soon, the forensic team shows up to take DNA samples and interview the witnesses. Before long, the accused is in court, lawyers screaming: "If the DNA doesn't fit, you must acquit!"

It probably wouldn't be that dramatic. But there are companies now that create a database of dog doo, called Poo Prints, and the dogs' DNA so the towns know who done it and who to ticket. The people checking are jokingly called "Poop Patrols." When the owners let their dogs leave something unsightly and unsanitary behind. It shouldn't be difficult to find a company to do this because a lot of people are stepping into this—not only the doo but the business of dog doo. They call the people who run these companies entre-manures. (Sorry.)

WHAT DOES AN ISRAELI COMPANY CALLED ASHPOOPIE DO? EXACTLY WHAT IT SOUNDS LIKE Here's the scoop on a unique pooper-scooper. According to *Nocamels.com,* a Ramat Gan-based company, Paulee Clean Tech gathers dog droppings (it may be better not to know how), and incinerates them. Then, in seconds, they're turned into odorless ash.

It may sound like a joke, but the company is serious enough to have received a grant from the **Bill & Melinda Gates Foundation.** They were interested in this eco-friendly company because it has the potential of reducing landfill waste. We don't want to know how much of it is you-know-what. Ash Poopie hopes to expand this to "human applications" and that too is more than we want to know.

PETS: CATS

HERE'S A JEWISH COMMERCIAL THAT DOESN'T PUSSYFOOT AROUND Over at the *Jewishindependent.com,* **Yori Yanover** decided to put his cat Sylvester to work helping to sell the website. He jokingly wrote that his cat "was hired for this role against type. The script originally called for a talking dog. Sylvester's not a dog. He's a thinker."

💻www.thejewishindependent.com/editors-pick/jewish-independent-cat-commercial

GO AHEAD AND PLAY WITH YOUR CAT—WHILE YOU'RE AWAY When your favorite felines aren't lying around practically cat-atonic, they want to play. *Israel21c.com* has reported on an Israeli invention coming soon that's a high-tech way to "adore, photograph, play with and feed" your cat. It's called Cat2See, and it's a cat-friendly webcam that you can control via your Smartphone. It'll do everything from making sure your cat gets food, to a tickling game on a stick that you can move around remotely for your kitty to chase.

You'll also be able to share the photos you take remotely with your (remote) friends. Why would you want to? Because that's what people do on the web. Before smartphones, someone once said that one day we will carry around a device that can access everything known to man... and all we'll do with it is argue with strangers and look at pictures of cats.

STARTUPS & DISCOVERIES
GOOD NEWS FROM ISRAEL—MAKING MONEY

WANT TO BE A BILLIONAIRE? GO TO ISRAEL! If becoming a mere millionaire is just too plebeian to endure, there are the ranks of billionaires you might consider joining. Even if you aren't born to super wealth, though, one of the best places for new billionaires to get their starts is Israel. The UK Centre for Policy Studies ranks it #2 for aspiring billionaires-to-be, with Hong Kong as the best.

This analysis features only billionaires listed by *Forbes* between 1996 and 2010, excluding those who were born with billions or acquired it through shady practices (sorry, Russia!).

Education was one of the most important factors in becoming wealthy. Despite famous college dropouts like Facebook's **Mark Zuckerberg** or Microsoft's **Bill Gates**, 86% had college degrees. Since Jerusalem has three of the world's 100 top universities—Hebrew University, the Technion, and the Weizmann Institute—you can start by going there.

Israel has 18 billionaires, six of them having made their money in information technology or biotechnology.

Bottom line: there's still room for you.

ISRAEL'S AMAZING SUCCESSES DESPITE...

The authors of *Start-up Nation* ask how Israel, with less than 8 million people, and no natural resources, surrounded by enemies bent on their destruction, and under constant attack, can produce more startup companies than Japan, India, Korea, Canada and the United Kingdom. Indeed, they have more companies on the NASDAQ than Korea, Japan, Singapore, India and all of Europe combined.

Israel is the number one place for entrepreneurs after America, and almost half of the world's top technology companies have bought startups or opened research and development in Israel. Meanwhile, Tel Aviv was ranked #2 in the world for startups by Startup Genome.

To name just a few of the accomplishments, the first PC anti-virus software was developed in Israel; an Israeli-developed algorithm enabled NASA to transmit images from Mars; the technology for AOL Instant Messenger was developed by four Israelis, and that's just for starters.

GOOD NEWS FROM ISRAEL— RESEARCH ON HEALTH

A PEEK INTO THE EXCITING RESEARCH GOING ON IN ISRAEL *Tiny Dynamo*, after pointing out that Israel attracts twice as much venture capital per capita as the next nearest recipient, America, listed some of the amazing accomplishments in Israel. When *Forbes* recently named the 10 best health tech companies, half of them were from Israel!

Here are just a few things they have accomplished or are working on to make us healthier and happier: Robotic spinal surgery, ingestible video camera so small it fits inside a pill, desalting the ocean, flash drive, anti-bacterial fabrics that reduce hospital infections, drip irrigation, a female equivalent to Viagra called Sheagra, "Ultrashape," a non-invasive liposuction to remove fat, a way to kill HIV cells, male birth control pills, using yellow water lilies for cancer treatment, creating a heart pacemaker from skin cells, a way to rehearse brain surgery before the real thing, studying the Israeli blind mole rat for a cure for cancer, a brain helmet for depression, and the development of a motorized shoe to stop people from falling.

Here's more of what they're working on.

THAT'S SHOCKING—SOUND WAVES MAY CURE IMPOTENCE Sound waves to cure impotence, technically called "extracorporeal shock wave therapy," consists of subjecting the recalcitrant member to 300 of the very same sound waves that have been successfully used to break up kidney stones.

Dr. Ilan Gruenwald, a neuro-urologist at Rambam Medical Center is the lead researcher of this treatment, which has been described as if a man was hitting his member "with a hammer." As if that wasn't unpleasant enough, it's not a one-shot thing. The treatment is done twice a week for three weeks. Then a pause, and it's repeated. For whatever reason, 30 percent of the patients reported that after a round of these shock treatments, Mr. Happy was back to his old tricks.

Some speculate that it might work because the sound waves encourage the growth of new blood vessels and improve circulation. You have to wonder, though, how they discovered this could work? And where did they find the men who were willing to be the first to try it?

CONSTIPATED? VIBRATING EGGS TO HELP LET OUR PEOPLE GO NBC reported that Israeli researchers with American funding have been testing a capsule that's sort of a vibrating egg, which people can use instead of laxatives for the same effect. It works six hours after insertion and massages people from the inside. As one reviewer delicately stated, it "frees up intestinal traffic jams."

Beyond that, you really don't want to know the details of the results, or the minor side effects that were occasionally reported. All you need to know is that if you need it right now, you'll have to wait. Which, if you need it, is probably what you're doing right now anyway. Waiting.

QUIT SMOKING BY SMELLING ROTTEN FISH & EGGS Israeli scientists at the Weizmann Institute of Science conducted tests that were successful in helping people cut down smoking by exposing them to disgusting smells, including cigarettes, while they sleep. The next day, smoking seems less attractive to them and they smoked far fewer cigarettes.

A BALLOON MAY KILL YOUR APPETITE An Israeli company has developed a pill that inflates like a balloon in your stomach, applying pressure on your stomach when it expands so that you feel full. Then, it's digested. While there are expanding balloons now based on the same principle, they require semi-surgery to insert, can pop, cause nausea, or intestinal blockage. One day, but not this year, you'll be able to pop one of these pills and not be hungry.

TOILET PAPER & DIAPERS—OUT OF JELLYFISH Most of us turn into jelly when we see them in the water, but Israeli researchers realize that jellyfish can be useful as "super absorbers." The *TimesofIsrael.com* reported that jellyfish are being studied for use in diapers, tampons, medical sponges and paper towels. Regardless, most of us still want to avoid them, which is why an Israeli company has developed the world's first jellyfish repellent.

A LOLLIPOP TO BANISH BAD BREATH *Israel21c.com* reported that an Israeli startup called "Breezy" has developed a sugar-free lollipop with slow-release microcapsules that scrape the tongue to remove the bacteria and food particles that cause halitosis. Most mouth fresheners only work for about an hour, and simply mask the problem. They claim this one can eradicate the problem and work for four hours. Its name is "Like" so you already know what their advertising slogan is going to say.

DOES SALT FROM THE DEAD SEA REALLY HELP PEOPLE? Or should we take the claims with a grain of salt? There are now dozens of "salt rooms" sprinkled throughout America where people sit in a salty room and pay money to...hmmm, breathe. They even sell Dead Sea salt scrubs now for dogs! As they say, some swear by it and some swear at it. They've been reported by believers to help people with arthritis, skin ailments, sinusitis, allergies, even wrinkling, plus certain Cystic Fibrosis symptoms. Some are impressed with the results; others dismiss it with a grain of (kosher) salt, saying it's a mostly unproven remedy for unspecified illnesses.

Still, entrepreneurs are carting the stuff in from Israel, where it is supposedly obtained from the Dead Sea, which may have been where **Jesus** was baptized. Still, historic does not mean healthy. At least there's no dispute that it's salty. The saltiest oceans on the planet are 3-6% salt, while the saline level here is between 28-35%. If you want to give it a try, you had better go quickly. Old-time comedian **George Burns** joked that when he was young, the Dead Sea was only sick, may come to pass. Ironically, the Dead Sea itself is dying and there may be nothing to ship from there by 2050.

SOLVING MAJOR PROBLEMS

ISRAELI DATES MAY PREVENT HEART DISEASE *The Jerusalem Post (jpost.com)* reported that it has been found that the nine varieties of dates in Israel may offer protection against cardiovascular disease. They're available on Israeli supermarket shelves, fresh or dried with "characteristics that help protect the heart." There are approximately 20 different varieties of dates grown throughout the world, but the Israeli ones are the best. What would you expect?

ISRAEL'S GOT YOUR BACK—OR WILL REPLACE IT Israel has developed replaceable synthetic spinal disks to fight back pain among people with a degenerative disk, as well as a minimally invasive systems for spinal correction, for example, to help someone with Scoliosis). They're also working on innovations that may help paraplegics walk.

THE END OF WORRYING ABOUT DATE RAPE DRUGS? The Israelis have developed a sensor to detect if someone has slipped date rape drug into a drink. Figures show that as many as 1 in 6 women will undergo rape or attempted rape in their lifetime, and possibly as many as 25% of those will be "facilitated" by a drug slipped into their drink without their knowledge.

Said *Salon.com* about inventions like this one: "The response is usually a resounding, 'Wow, great idea!' But how cool would it be if the response were, 'Why ever would we need that?'"

"KISS" CANCER GOODBYE Mistletoe can be used for more than just facilitating a bit of smooching at Christmas. A study in Haifa found that mistletoe extract helped stabilize patients suffering from advanced colon or lung cancer when chemotherapy was no longer working.

SWALLOW GOLD TO SEE IF SOMEONE HAS CANCER Early tests have been 90% effective in establishing when someone has cancer on the tongue or larynx by having them gargle with a mixture of nanoparticles of gold. *Haaretz.com* reported that the suspected cancer cells are painted with the gold, and then scanned.

ALZHEIMER'S RESEARCH SHOULD NOT BE FORGOTTEN There's a great deal of ongoing research on Alzheimer's in Israel, perhaps because of their aging population. One study is questioning whether using bursts of gentle electricity will slow Alzheimer's progression. Another is looking into ways to possibly reverse Alzheimer's altogether. There are more than 10 promising studies ongoing now, so hopefully Alzheimer's is one problem they'll one day be able to forget.

~✡~✡~✡~

CHAI TECH

THE ANTI-SOCIAL NETWORK Facebook is now so popular that virtually everyone has dozens of "friends," many of whom they couldn't identify if they ran into them at a party. But what about "frenemies" or people we do know but don't want to meet at certain times? Like ever.

We may not have deleted them from our Facebook friends list for many reasons. Maybe we don't need the drama of their discovery that they're no longer our BFFs (Best Friends Forever.) But there are also people we've friended and know and like but we just don't necessarily want to run into at certain times. Like former spouses when we're with a new love. Or our boss at the beach when we've called in sick. Or anyone when we're recovering from plastic surgery.

Now, having these people you want to avoid on Facebook can actually be useful. Jaffa entrepreneur **Udi Dagan** has invented a unique application in anti-social networking. "Split," a free app, offers "Real Time Alerts" ("Yikes—he's near,") "Event Notifications" ("Hope she's not at the party,") "Danger Zone Pointers" ("uh uh, watch out for her,") "Who's There" ("Don't want to go to that party,") and "Who With" ("Can't stand him.") It will even give you warnings if one of your "friends" is within 1,000 feet of you—and plot evasive maneuvers for you so you can escape your friend quickly.

Dagan claims the average user of the application has between four to nine people on their do-not-want list. If this app takes off, people will be staying away in droves from their friends.

TELL KIDS THIS
AND THEY'LL UNDERSTAND HANUKKAH!

A mother was trying to explain to her tech-savvy son about the miracle of Hanukkah, but the kid didn't understand. So she told him: "Imagine you charge your phone, and it lasts for eight days."

CHAPTER 15
SERIOUSLY: DEFENSE, PREJUDICE AND THE THIRD REICH

✡

DEFENSE
WHO'S IN THE IDF?
(ISRAEL DEFENSE FORCES)

13 Gamal Abdul Nasser, the former President of Egypt, after he lost the Six-day War, complained that it was unfair. "Israel has over two million Jews and we don't have any."

Israel has soldiers from many nations. According to *TheDailyBeast.com,* Israel is one of four countries that lets Americans serve in their military. As a result, about 1,000 of the 4,000 non-Israeli-born troops in the IDF are from the US, taking advantage of the right-of-return law.

Don't expect to see any blue-and-white recruiting stations in the US. It's illegal for Israel to recruit within the states, so people have to go to Israel to join. One American who did wrote a hilarious book about it: *The 188th Crybaby Brigade: A Skinny Jewish Kid from Chicago Fights Hezbollah* by **Joel Chasnoff.**

BILL MAHER'S HILARIOUS TAKE ON "OPERATION PROTECTIVE EDGE"

"Israelis agreed to a 5-hour cease-fire so the Gazans could get supplies. How Jewish is that? 'We're going to attack you—but first, you should eat'."

WHO WAS THE IDF'S MOST FAMOUS FIGHTER—AND VICTIM? Karola Ruth Siegel—now known as **Dr. Ruth Westheimer**, or more often simply Dr. Ruth—came to Palestine from Switzerland after she had lost her parents in the Holocaust. Like those in similar situations, she joined the Haganah, an underground Jewish military organization.

Her small size helped mask her as a sniper, and she turned out to be incredibly accurate at throwing hand grenades as well. "Even today I can load a Stern automatic rifle in a single minute, blindfolded," she told interviewer **Tom Foreman.**

Her skills were badly needed, but her military career was cut short when she was seriously injured on her 20th birthday. An Arab shell from Jordan exploded at her feet and she was thrown 20 feet. "My legs were almost ripped off from cannon ball shrapnel," she said of her sniper career in her autobiography, *All in a Lifetime: An Autobiography*. Three others were killed instantly, and many more were wounded in the attack. "The strangest thing was that all I could think about was whether there might be some blood on the brand-new shoes I had just gotten for my birthday," she recalled.

HOLD YOUR NOSE—SKUNK SPRAY IS BEING USED FOR DEFENSE Israel has developed—and has been using—stink bombs to disperse crowds and punish protesters and demonstrators. *The Economist,* subtitling their story "a whiff from hell," described the noxious smell as "like raw sewage mixed with putrefying cow's carcass."

"Skunk" has no side effects, although it is hard to get the smell off the clothes or person who has been sprayed. American police were reportedly interested in this liquid which was developed by the Israeli police. And if anyone here gets sprayed, they'll probably think the whole thing stinks.

HOW TO GET WOMEN TO WANT TO FIGHT

Just about everyone knows that women fight in the Israeli army. But Brooklyn-bred comedian **Elayne Boosler** joked about what could make women in the army actually want to kill the enemy.

She says they definitely would if the General just said to them: "See the enemy over there? I heard them talking. They say you look fat in your uniform."

PALESTINIANS [LIGHT]

THE "FUNNY" THING ABOUT PALESTINIANS IN ISRAEL There are many variations of this, but in this one, **Bibi Netanyahu** is speaking before the UN Security Council. "Three thousand years ago, **Moses** parted the Red Sea to lead our people into the promised land. But first, he took off his clothes and swam around a bit. But when he got back to shore, he couldn't find his clothes because they had been stolen by the Arabs."

The Arab delegations all started shouting at him "Liar. Why is it that every time something gets stolen you blame the Arabs! There even weren't any Arabs in that area at that period of time!"

Bibi said: "Thank you. That's exactly the point I wanted to make in my speech."

Golda Meir, the first and only female Prime Minister of Israel, said basically the same thing but without humor to the *Sunday Times* in 1969 when she said there was no such thing as Palestinians. "When was there an independent Palestinian people with a Palestinian state? It was either southern Syria before the First World War, and then it was a Palestine state including Jordan. It was not as though there was a Palestinian people in Palestine considering itself a Palestinian people, and we came and threw them out and took their country away from them. They did not exist."

JEWS VS. PALESTINIANS...AND A FLY IN A COFFEE CUP This one has been going around the Internet for years in different forms, but here's the latest (until the next version). The Israeli sells the coffee to the Frenchman, the cup to the Italian, and uses the profit to develop a device that prevents future flies from falling into coffee.

The Palestinian blames the Israeli for the fly falling into his coffee, protests the act to the UN, takes a loan from the European Union to buy a new cup of coffee, uses the money to purchase explosives,, and then blows up the coffee house where the Italian and Frenchman (Chinese, German and Russian) are all trying to explain to the Israeli that he should give his cup of tea to the Palestinian.

JOAN RIVERS SAID THAT NOSE JOBS WOULD BRING PEACE TO THE MIDDLE EAST

"I think every Palestinian should get a nose job, because once somebody has had a nose job, they won't fight because they're scared their new nose will get broken," joked Joan Rivers. She told an interviewer on Channel 10 in Israel: "I think we should send over every great Jewish plastic surgeon doctor, fix their noses, and there'll be peace in the Middle East" reported jewcy.com.

JUST SO YOU SHOULD KNOW

Howard Stern is known for being controversial, but he was right-on during "Operation Protective Edge." "If you're anti-Israel, then you're anti-American. It's the only democracy over there. It's the only friend we have who's willing to fight and stand up for what's right."

Benjamin Netanyahu has been widely quoted as saying that: "Israel uses its missiles to protect its citizens, while Hamas uses their citizens to protect their missiles."

He also once said, "If the Arabs put down their weapons today, there would be no more violence. If the Jews put down their weapons today, there would be no more Israel."

PREJUDICE

FOUR BITS OF GOOD NEWS ABOUT NON-JEWS' ATTITUDES TOWARD JEWS First, **Jules Farber** once jokingly wrote, "The time is at hand when the wearing of a prayer shawl and skullcap will not bar a man from the White House. Unless, of course, the man is Jewish."

Seriously, a Jew has a lot better chance of being President now than he/ she did years ago. Gallup took a survey in 1947 on how many people would vote for a Jew for President. Less than half (47%) said they would. In 2012, 91% said they would vote for a Jewish President.

Secondly, Jews (and supporters) were justifiably very upset when a 2014 Pew Poll showed that 93% of the Arab world harbored anti-Semitic views. But look at it this way: at least 7% *haven't* been brainwashed about Jews. And when you think of how many Arabs there are, that's a lot of enemies we *don't* have.

Next, this may be a stretch, but in *Judaism for Dummies,* they point out that there's no such thing as "anti-Semites." They write that "Semites" includes all the descendants of Shem, the oldest son of Noah. That includes Jews, Arabs, and other tribes. Since so many Arabs hate Jews, anti-Semitism makes no sense; they don't hate themselves.

Finally, here's a cheerful thought. "Americans Say Jews Are The Coolest," was the headline in the *theatlantic.com.* A July 2014 Pew Poll of American attitudes toward other faiths on their "warmth" or "coolness" toward Jews, Catholics, Hindus, Muslims, evangelicals, atheists and more, found that the respondents were most likely to feel warmly toward Jews. Kind of makes you feel warm and fuzzy inside.

WHO WOULD HAVE EXPECTED IT? FIVE SURPRISING PEOPLE WHO WEREN'T ANTI-SEMITIC

NAPOLEON The Little Corporal gave full citizenship to French Jewry in 1806, but it wasn't for altruistic reasons—he wanted their support. Whatever, it was better than the kick in the tuchis other

Frenchmen were giving to the Jews because of increasing hostility at the time toward Jewish moneylenders.

FRANK SINATRA "Old Blue Eyes" gave a lot of green to Israel. This Italian Catholic singer fought anti-Semitism whenever he could—sometimes doing it his way. For example, he punched someone out who made an anti-Jewish comment in front of him at a party. He also walked out on the christening of his own son when the priest refused to allow one of his Jewish friends to be the child's godfather. Most helpful, he made a ten-minute film to oppose anti-Semitism at the end of World War II.

⌨ See http://tinyurl.com/jd3v2pe

MARTIN LUTHER KING Award-winning investigative reporter **Richard Behar** uncovered details of a dinner in Cambridge, Massachusetts in 1968, shortly before **Martin Luther King** was assassinated. When someone started attacking Israel, King interrupted the speaker: "'Don't talk like that. When people criticize Zionists, they mean Jews. You're talking anti-Semitism."

MARLON BRANDO While he was often depicted as mumbling, he was loud and clear in his support of the Jews. He felt that it was the Jews who helped him get started early in his career, especially the famous acting coach, Stella Adler, who not only taught him to act but let him live with her and her family when he was starting out.

During the two years starting in 1946 that he was in the Broadway play about the birth of Israel, *A Flag Is Born,* he continually gave money to the Irgun, a Zionist group which rescued European Jews and worked to establish Israel as an independent sovereign nation.

BRIGHAM YOUNG Here's a shocker: According to *Jewishmag.com,* **Brigham Young**, President of the Church of Jesus Christ of Latter-day Saints, known as the Mormons, donated land to create the first Jewish cemetery in Salt Lake City.

THE "MAGIC" YARMULKE THAT KEEPS JEWS FROM BEING ATTACKED It's come to this. Jews in many places have to wear near-invisible yarmulkes called a "Magic Kippa," [sic] to hide the fact that they're wearing skullcaps so they won't be shunned, spit at, or even attacked. Designed by an Israeli barber, the synthetic hair costs around $50—the one with real hair is $70 more—and blends in naturally with the man's own hair, assuming he has some. The nearly invisible kippah which clips on to the real hair can be washed, brushed, and even dyed to match a man's real hair color.

Sadly, but not surprising, AP reported that most buyers were from France and Belgium. Unfortunately, they'll probably sell well elsewhere and become increasingly popular—and necessary. Let's hope the Israeli inventor never becomes a millionaire.

FAKE OUT

OH, THE IRONY! SCIENTIST STEPHEN HAWKING BOYCOTTED ISRAEL, BUT HE CAN'T TALK WITHOUT HIS SPEECH MACHINE—DEVELOPED IN ISRAEL! "How can a man as brilliant as **[Stephen] Hawking** boycott Israel when it makes the microchip that enables him to talk?" asked **Douglas Murphy** in the *Daily Mail*. Yes, without the speech device made in Israel—a computer Intel Core i7-based communication system which runs on a chip designed by IsraelAll—Hawking would be unable to communicate with the world.

Wrote Murphy: "Even the brightest people can make fools of themselves, he has now done something which is beyond stupid."

Hawking, whose motor neuron disease has left him in a wheelchair and unable to speak, boycotted the prestigious "Facing Tomorrow" conference. Although he later gave some unconvincing excuse, he probably boycotted it because it was hosted by **Shimon Peres**, then President of Israel. Added Murray, "Perhaps Professor Hawking should reflect on what it would mean [to him] if he truly committed himself to a boycott of Israel."

AND MORE IRONY: AL-QAIDA UNKNOWINGLY USED AN ISRAELI COMPANY TO KEEP THEIR E-MAIL SECURE! The Middle East Media Research Institute discovered that Al Qaida's media organization was keeping their e-mail private by using Safe-mail—which is owned and operated by Secure Information Technologies Ltd., a privately owned company *registered in Israel! The Jerusalem Post (jpost.com)* reported that once the terrorists found out, they said the program could not be trusted, and they dropped it, using their own encryption software.

Oh good—now we'll be able to read their e-mails.

ANTI-SEMITES MAY BE SPEAKING YIDDISH WHEN THEY CALL JEWS "KIKES" If someone calls a Jew a "kike," they may be speaking Yiddish without realizing it. Wikipedia says the derogatory slur referring to Jews may come from the Yiddish word "circle," because non-English-speaking Jews immigrating to the Americas would sign papers with a circle instead of an X.

ANTI-ISRAEL PRESS

CAN YOU IMAGINE THE WORLD PRESS IF IT WAS THE *ISRAELIS* WHO HAD KILLED THE PUPPIES? Someone once tweeted that if a tree falls in the woods and there's no one to hear it, is it still Israel's fault. (And you can be sure the press will report it.) One of the most horrifying stories about what some Palestinians did against Israelis was barely mentioned in the non-Jewish press. But can you imagine the world outrage if it had been the *Israelis* who had thrown and killed newborn puppies at the Palestinians?

Israellycool.com and *jewsnews.co.il* and only a few small Internet news sites reported that on March 2014, Arab residents of Abu Dis near Jerusalem threw four bags with *live* puppies at the border police. The stunned and horrified police could hear the puppies whimpering as they died.

So why hasn't the world reported on this one? Where is the outrage? If it had been the other way around, it would have been reported in every major (and minor) newspaper in the world.

Tapzit News Agency reported on the story of a 15-year-old Palestinian boy with severe burns and shrapnel injuries from a rocket launching pad set up in a neighborhood in northern Gaza. He was treated in an Israeli hospital—so Israel treated a kid who got injured when he tried to kill Israelis! And they also even once treated the Prime Minister of Hamas for a heart condition.

As one Israeli posted to *quora.com:* "Our doctors don't ask who these people are. Some of them might be rebels...some of them might even be Al-Qaeda.... Many times we help those who will not think twice before killing us..."

HOW THE PRESS MISREPRESENTS ISRAEL A young girl visiting a zoo was suddenly grabbed by an African lion who tried to pull her through the bars into his cage. Risking his life, an Israeli tourist who was present leaped forward, jumped into the cage, and pulled the lion away from the child, saving her. The headline the next day in the British newspapers:

ISRAELI ASSAULTS AFRICAN
IMMIGRANT AND STEALS ITS LUNCH

THE BDS [OR BS] MOVEMENT

THE BOYCOTT OF ISRAELI PRODUCTS AND WHY IT MAY NOT BE A REAL THREAT The boycott of Israel, called the BDS movement, supposedly stands for "Boycott, Divestment & Sanctions," but some have said BDS should stand for "Baksheesh, Dishonesty, and Sanctimoniousness."

The headline in a *TimesofIsrael.com* blog by **Jonah Balfour** best explains why he believes a boycott is not a serious threat to Israel. "It's already too late for the boycotters." But that's just one reason the decade-old boycott of business, academic and cultural Israeli institutions is (hopefully) not going to achieve its goal.

Balfour points out that Israel is already too integrated into the global economy, especially in the tech sphere. People can't boycott certain brands even if they want to. For example, the single largest tech employer is Intel. "How can anyone even begin to approach a boycott...responsible for 80% of all CPUs in computers today?"

The other reason the attempts to get consumers to avoid Israeli

146   Was Elvis Jewish?

products have been mostly unsuccessful is because it's hard to identify "Israeli" products. Israel has a few recognizable international brands. SodaStream is one, as is a publicly traded company called Teva Pharmaceutical Industries, which makes generic drugs—the opposite of identifiable branding.

Finally, he optimistically concludes that while Israel faces serious challenges: "An economic boycott led by the BDS movement is not one of them."

Even if it happily won't cripple Israel, what should people do about the boycott? As **Alan Dershowitz,** a Harvard professor of law for over 50 years, said of universities espousing Israeli boycotts: "If universities divest from Israel, alumni should divest from those universities. You do fight economic fire with economic fire. Fight back—very very vigorously."

NOTE: Several states are pushing bills to block aid to public universities using taxpayers' dollars boycotting Israel... thereby boycotting the boycotters.

EIGHT CREEPS WHO PUSHED FOR BOYCOTTING ISRAEL OK, in fairness to them, some musicians won't play Israel for reasons other than anti-Zionist convictions. Before he performed in Israel, singer **Moby** explained: "Most artists just don't want to deal with it. It's much easier for them to release a statement that they won't be appearing in Israel 'for reasons of conscience' rather than to say their lives are being threatened and they're frightened." Still, you might want to think twice (or ten times) before supporting these people by paying money for tickets.

Alice Walker, most famous for writing *The Color Purple,* is blind in one eye from a BB gun accident caused by her brother when she was young). But she is now totally blind to the truth. In an open letter, she tried to get singer-songwriter **Alicia Keys** to cancel her Israel performance and join the boycott of Israel. Walker has been a long-time activist for Palestinian rights and visited Gaza in 2008.

Honorable mention goes to Pink Floyd member **Roger Waters** (who also tried to persuade Alicia Keys not to perform in Israel), **Danny Glover** (super creep championing BDS), **Stevie Wonder** (he pulled out of a benefit for the "Friends of the Israel Defense Forces"), **Elvis Costello** (cancelled his concert in Israel), **Carlos Santana, Jon Bon Jovi, Eric Burden** (with the "Animals," where some think he belongs).

MORE HOLLYWOOD CREEPS There should be a "**Vanessa Redgrave** Hollywood Award for Idiocy and Anti-Semitism." She was an outspoken champion for the Palestinians, and the Jewish Defense League tried to prevent her from receiving an award for Best Supporting Actress. When she received the Oscar anyway, she called those against her "Zionist hoodlums" during her Oscar acceptance speech.

The recipient of this apocryphal award now would be **Emma Thompson** (*Saving Mr. Banks,* etc.,) who tried to ban an Israeli theater company from performing at a Shakespeare festival in England. Runners up could be **Javier Bardem** and **Penelope Cruz,** who signed a public letter denouncing Israel when it was trying to defend itself during "Operation Protective Edge." And **Selena Gomez,** who sent out an Instagram post "praying for the people of Gaza," leading **Joan Rivers** to say: "Let's see if she can spell Palestinian."

A SURPRISING (NON-JEWISH) STAR WHO CONDEMNED THE BOYCOTTERS After **Javier Bardem** and **Penelope Cruz's** anti-Semitic vitriol, **Jon Voight,** best known for his role in *Midnight Cowboy,* and for being the (estranged) father of actress **Angelina Jolie,** came out with a surprising denunciation of Bardem and Cruz for "inciting anti-Semitism all over the world....

Aish.com wrote: "....You had a great responsibility to use your celebrity for good. Instead, you have defamed the only democratic country of goodwill in the Middle East: Israel. You should hang your heads in shame." And on another occasion. he said: "Instead of telling Hamas to stop sending rockets into Israel aimed at its civilian population, they say Israel has to stop killing civilians. What a travesty of justice."

THE THIRD REICH
HITLER

WHY HITLER'S "MEIN KAMPF" IS ONE OF THE MOST POPULAR E-BOOKS TODAY Certainly no one would buy **Adolf Hitler's** definitive book for its literary value. One reviewer said it should have been called *Mein Krampf* (or *My Cramp*) because of its "constipated" style. Others have suggested a title reflecting the opposite problem. According to *Adolf Hitler: A Psychological Interpretation of his Views...*, the second volume contained "an estimated 164,000 errors in grammar and syntax.

Even so, the 99-cent unabridged 528-page e-book has become enormously popular in this country. Author and journalist **Chris Faraone** at *The Guardian* attributed it to e-books allowing people's curiosity to be sated privately, as with smut and romance novels. "People might not have wanted to buy [it] or have it delivered to their home or displayed on their living room bookshelf, let alone get spotted reading it on a subway, but ...digital copies can be quietly perused then dropped into a folder or deleted."

But however many idiots (or anti-Semites, same thing) have purchased it in the belief that they can read it in secret, **Mary Elizabeth Williams** at *Salon* reminds us that no online purchase is really private. She quotes the *Guardian* as saying: "The person opposite you on the tube may not know you're following Der Fuehrer on your Kindle, but Amazon...does." She concludes that you should enjoy your illusions of privacy until your "recommendations scare the [heck] out of you."

Serves them right.

WHATEVER HAPPENED TO HITLER'S DOG? It's hard to picture **Hitler** as being close to anyone, but Alsatian dog, Blondi, slept with him in the bedroom of his bunker. In fact, Hitler liked Blondi so much that he killed her.

When Hitler saw that it was the end for them all, he began worrying about the efficacy of the cyanide capsules he had ready to use at the end. So to be sure they would work, he had them tested on his beloved Blondi.

NAZI ERA

IS IT TRUE THAT ALL DANES WORE A YELLOW STAR WHEN THE JEWS WERE ORDERED TO DO SO? When the Jews were ordered to put on a yellow armband during the war in Denmark, it's generally believed that all the Danes—even the King himself—put on an armband so the Jews wouldn't stand out. This little bit of "history" appeared in both the novel and movie version of *Exodus*.

But it wasn't true. It was a propaganda piece put out by a PR spin doctor at the National Denmark-America Association. Even so, Denmark treated Jews better than some of the other European countries.

FOR ONLY THREE MILLION DOLLARS YOU COULD HAVE PURCHASED "SCHINDLER'S LIST" ON EBAY "What better way to honor the selflessness of **Oskar Schindler**, who went broke saving thousands of Jews from extermination, than by giving millions of dollars to a rich guy for a piece of paper?"asked **Dan Amira** in *New York* magazine.

He was referring to the 3 million dollar price tag someone put on eBay for a private copy of Schindler's List. Was it worth $3 million? Well, it turns out that there were actually *four* lists and this was just one of them, and some even questioned the authenticity of the original list. Apparently, the public decided it wasn't worth the three million (or perhaps three cents) because the auctioneer received no bids.

TWO SURPRISING COMMENTS ABOUT JEWS DURING THE NAZI ERA *Jewnews.com* reported that **Robin Williams** once said: "I was on this German talk show and this woman said to me, 'Mr. Williams, why do you think there is not so much comedy in Germany?' And I said 'Did you ever think you killed all the funny people?'"

GUESS WHO? The person who made this pro-Jewish comment is one of the last people in the world you would have expected to say it: "The Jewish people, no matter where they are, become the best in the world." He was a major officer at Auschwitz, the man who determined who would live—and who he wanted to experiment on—**Josef Mengele.**

THE HORRENDOUS HOLOCAUST STORY YOU NEVER HEARD On May 3, 1945, a large German ocean liner called the Cap Arcona, which was filled with thousands of concentration camp prisoners, was accidentally bombed by the British Royal Airforce. They mistakenly believed that it was filled with Nazis trying to escape.

Around 4,500 former concentration camp victims — most Jewish —were killed by the bombing. The British even shot those in the water who were trying to escape.

The British attempted to cover this story up for the past 70 years by trying to keep the records of the "friendly fire" bombing sealed. But popular professor and lecturer, **Dr. Robert Watson**, of Lynn University in Florida, uncovered the story and turned it into an extraordinary book, *The Nazi Titanic* (available at amazon.com).

~~~✡~~~

ANNE FRANK

UNBELIEVABLE! MANY AMERICANS DON'T KNOW WHO ANNE FRANK WAS In case you're one of those young people who don't know who **Anne Frank** was, she kept a detailed diary from June 1942 to August 1944 while hiding from the Nazis during the German occupation of the Netherlands. Of the eight people she hid with, seven were found and killed. And she died of typhoid at the Bergen-Belsen concentration camp at the age of 15.

In "The Incredibly Depressing Answers College Students Gave When Asked What the Holocaust Was," (you don't want to know from most of their answers), one person replied that he didn't know who Anne Frank was because he had never read the book.

Another admitted that he had confused her for **Helen Keller**, the deaf, dumb and blind American author and political activist.

FOUR SURPRISING THINGS YOU DIDN'T KNOW ABOUT ANNE FRANK

Had **Anne Frank** lived, she would recently have celebrated her 85th birthday.

She didn't actually write in a diary. It was an autograph book (which she named "Kitty") that she received for her 13th birthday.

In 2012, the Church of Jesus Christ of Latter-Day Saints, aka, the Mormons, posthumously baptized by proxy Anne Frank as a Mormon.

You can actually see Anne today in very brief surviving film footage. Her neighbors were getting married, and she stuck her head out the window to watch them.

⌨ www.jewsnews.co.il/2013/06/24/video-the-only-surviving-film-footage-of-anne-frank

THE JAPANESE ARE OBSESSED WITH ANNE FRANK
JTA.org, in a piece by **Alain Lewkowicz,** revealed that the Japanese are obsessed with **Anne Frank.** Indeed, some young Japanese consider her their "soul mate." They've heard about her in their Japanese manga comic book adaptations of her diary, in anime cartoon films, and in excerpts from her diary, which are read in many classes.

In terms of absolute numbers of copies of the book sold, Japan is second only to the United States. It's also the only East Asian country with statues and a museum in memory of Anne Frank. The *JewishJournal.com* said more Japanese tourists visit the Anne Frank House annually in Amsterdam than Israelis: 30,000, about 5,000 visitors more than the number from Israel.

Why? Besides the exposure to her story, they're obsessed with young women in Japan. If it seems hard to fathom their interest, as one person posted on the Internet, "It's hard for us to explain, but then they find us a bit nuts, too."

That's for sure!

JUST SO YOU SHOULD KNOW

Marcel Marceau is best known as a mime, but he was also a painter whose artwork is worth a lot of money. He became a mime while trying to help keep children quiet who were attempting to escape during the war.

Writer **Bernard Malamud** once said: "If you ever forget you're a Jew, a Gentile will remind you."

Columnist **Liz Smith**, after reviewing **Frederic Morton's** book on Vienna, poetically wrote about the eve of WWI: "This was a world of music, drama, fashion, and full-dress uniforms. It was all going along pretty well for Austrians of all stripe, but at the turn of the century, a baby boy was born to the **Hitlers** of Vienna."

CHAPTER 16
WORDS OF WISDOM [kvell time]

WHAT PEOPLE HAVE SAID ABOUT JEWS

WHAT PRESIDENTS AND PRIME MINISTERS HAVE SAID ABOUT ISRAEL AND JEWS

- "Israel was not created in order to disappear—Israel will endure and flourish. It is the child of hope and home of the brave. It can neither be broken by adversity nor demoralized by success. It carries the shield of democracy and it honors the sword of freedom." **(John Kennedy)**

- "I had faith in Israel before it was established, I have in it now. I believe it has a glorious future before it—not just another sovereign nation, but as an embodiment of the great ideals of our civilization." **(Harry S. Truman)**

- "I will insist that the Hebrews have done more to civilize man than any other nation."(Letter from **John Adams** to **Thomas Jefferson**)

- President **Abraham Lincoln** said that restoring the Jews to their "natural" home in Palestine was "a noble dream and one shared by many Americans." The President also said his chiropodist was a Jew who "has so many times 'put me upon my feet' that I would have no objection to giving his countrymen 'a leg up.'" He also said, "I myself have a great regard for Jews."

- **Richard Nixon** said: "Americans admire a people who can scratch a desert and produce a garden. The Israelis have shown qualities that Americans identify with: guts, patriotism, idealism, a passion for freedom. I have seen it. I know. I believe that." (In private, he also said a lot of miserable anti-Semitic things.)

- **Winston Churchill**, former Prime Minister of the United Kingdom, historian, writer, orator ("We have nothing to fear but fear itself,") artist, Nobel Prize winner and the man often thought to be one of the greatest wartime leaders of the 20th century, said this about the Jews. "Some people like the Jews and some do not. But no thoughtful man can deny the fact they are, beyond any question, the most formidable and remarkable race which has appeared in the world."

- And finally, not every past president has good things to say about Israel. Former President **Jimmy Carter** said: "The United States is squandering international prestige and goodwill and intensifying global anti-American terrorism by unofficially condoning or abetting the Israeli confiscation and colonization of Palestinian territories."

THREE MORE GREAT QUOTES ABOUT ISRAEL

- "No country in the history of the world has ever contributed more to humankind and accomplished more for its people in so brief a period of time as Israel has done since its relatively recent rebirth in 1948."
  (Alan Dershowitz)

- "Israel is slightly smaller than New Jersey. **Moses** in effect led the tribes of Israel out of the District of Columbia, parted the Chesapeake Bay near Annapolis, and wandered for forty years in Delaware."
  (P. J. O'Rourke)

- "A nation defending its citizens against terrorist bombings and a military and diplomatic onslaught by an array of Arab foes is practicing survival, not genocide."
  (Jack Schwartz, scientist)

FIVE TERRIFIC STATEMENTS ABOUT ISRAEL BY GOLDA MEIR

- "It is true we have won all our wars, but we have paid for them. We don't want victories anymore."

- "Let me tell you something that we Israelis have against Moses. He took us 40 years through the desert in order to bring us to the one spot in the Middle East that has no oil!"

- "We have always said that in our war with the Arabs we had a secret weapon—no alternative."

- "We can forgive the Arabs for killing our children. We cannot forgive them for forcing us to kill their children."

- "We will only have peace with the Arabs when they love their children more than they hate us."

APARTHEID, RACISM, BOYCOTTS & THE GARBAGE THEY SPEW

WHY ISRAEL IS NOT AN APARTHEID NATION OR RACIST STATE Said columnist **Charles Krauthammer** about the apartheid calumny: "If there is one minority in the Middle East that enjoys the rule of law, and protection, and democracy, it is Arabs in Israel. One out of every five Israelis is a Palestinian. Overwhelmingly, they're Muslim. There are Arabs in the government, in the Supreme Court, in all walks of life, in the universities. There's actually affirmative action if you're a Palestinian in the universities. And to compare that, in any way, with the systematic discrimination against black Africans in South Africa is truly appalling..."

THE HYPOCRISY OF THE BOYCOTTS AGAINST ACADEMIC INSTITUTIONS (& ISRAEL) Larry Summers, former President of Harvard, speaking on the *Charlie Rose* Show about the boycott against Israel, said: "The idea that of all the countries in the world that might be thought to have human rights abuses...inappropriate foreign policies, that... there's only one that is worthy of boycott... Israel...is...beyond outrageous."

THE ARAB-ISRAELI CONFLICT

AMAZINGLY, THIS WAS WRITTEN ABOUT ISRAEL'S PROBLEMS 50 YEARS AGO It could have been written today. **Eric Hoffer,** a longshoreman/ philosopher/writer, and author of the classic *The True Believer,* wrote this in the *Los Angeles Times* almost 50 years ago: How little things have changed!

..."Things permitted to other nations are forbidden to the Jews. Other nations drive out thousands, even millions of people and there is no refugee problem. Russia did it, Poland and Czechoslovakia did it. Turkey threw out a million Greeks and Algeria a million Frenchman. Indonesia threw out heaven knows how many Chinese and no one says a word about refugees.

"But in the case of Israel, the displaced Arabs have become eternal refugees. Everyone insists that Israel must take back every single one.

"There is a cry of outrage all over the world when people die in Vietnam or when two blacks are executed in Rhodesia. But when **Hitler** slaughtered Jews no one demonstrated against him. The Jews are alone in the world. If Israel survives, it will be solely because of Jewish efforts. And Jewish resources. Yet at this moment, Israel is our only reliable and unconditional ally. We can rely more on Israel than Israel can rely on us....

"I have a premonition that will not leave me; as it goes with Israel so will it go with all of us. Should Israel perish, the Holocaust will be upon us all."

ALAN DERSHOWITZ SHOWED HOW THE PROBLEM IS THE SAME TODAY When **Alan Dershowitz** was interviewed by **Curt Schleier** for the *forward.com,* Dershowitz said: "Remember that old ad, 'This is your brain. This is your brain on drugs'? Well, this is your brain, and this is your brain when Jews are involved, and the Jewish nation is involved. Then all bets are off. Equality goes out the window. Decency goes out the window.

What should be obvious in any other context is not when Israel is involved.... What Israel does is perfectly rational and reasonable in any other country, but a double standard is applied to Israel...."

Simon Deng, once a Sudanese slave, said: "The UN has itself become a tool against Israel. For over 50 years, 82 percent of the UN General Assembly emergency meetings have been about condemning one state—Israel. **Hitler** couldn't have been made happier!

"There are peoples who suffer from the UN's anti-Israelism even more than the Israelis. I belong to one of those people.... The UN is concerned about the so-called Palestinian refugees.... Meanwhile, my people, ethnically cleansed, murdered and enslaved, are relatively ignored.... My people have been driven off the front pages because of the exaggerations about Palestinian suffering. ....Look at the situation of the Copts in Egypt, the Christians in Iraq, and Nigeria, and Iran, the Hindus and Baha'is who suffer from Islamic oppression. The Sikhs.... We are ignored, we are abandoned. So that the big lie against the Jews can go forward.

"I have been to Israel five times visiting the Sudanese refugees.... In Israel, black Sudanese, Christian, and Muslim, were welcomed and treated like human beings....

"Is Israel a racist state? The answer is 'absolutely not'. Israel is a state of people who are the colours of the rainbow....."As a friend of Israel, I bring you the news that my President, the President of the Republic of South Sudan, **Salva Kiir**—publicly stated that the South Sudan Embassy in Israel will be built...in Jerusalem, the eternal capital of the Jewish people....AM YISRAEL CHAI !

"The people of Israel live!"

PULITZER PRIZE-WINNING JOURNALIST LAWRENCE WRIGHT BELIEVES THINGS WILL GET BETTER IN THE MIDDLE EAST Lawrence Wright, Pulitzer-prize winning author of *The Looming Tower* and also the author of a wonderful anti-Scientology book, *Going Clear,* is also the prize-winning author of *Thirteen Days in September: Carter, Begin, and Sadat at Camp David.* As a middle-East specialist, when he was interviewed by the *forward.com,* he presented a more sanguine view of Israel's future than most.

Can peace prevail? "I grew up in the American South and watched the Civil Rights movement. Now we have a black president. I grew up in the Cold War; it seemed like the world was going to be frozen forever until it was destroyed. Now the Soviet Union is gone.... Apartheid is gone. And now the tyrants of the Arab world are being rolled aside one by one.

"So don't tell me things can't change. Things can change and things can change for the better. And it can happen in the Middle East. It's not an impossible problem; it's a political problem. Political people will have to solve it, but they'll have to find the courage to sell it to their own people."

PALESTINIANS

INVESTIGATIVE REPORTER RICHARD BEHAR ON ISRAELI TREATMENT OF ARABS "The Jews came [to Israel] carrying farm tools. They didn't steal land; they overpaid for it from Palestinian urban notables and absentee Arab landlords living in other countries. Many Arab tenant farmers benefitted as well; for the first time in their lives, they were paid decent wages by their new (Jewish) employers. ...As for genocide and ethnic cleansing, if Israelis are engaged in those acts they should win the Nobel Prize for the gang that couldn't shoot straight. Israeli-Arab and Palestinian populations are growing, not shrinking.

"But is there discrimination in Israel? Absolutely—just like in America and elsewhere, between a majority population and its minorities. But...there are active affirmative action policies and programs to help Arabs catch up, not to mention high-tech projects to bring Arabs into Israel's 'Start-Up Nation.'

PALESTINIANS? COMEDIAN SAYS THERE ARE NO SUCH PEOPLE The following was written and widely distributed in viral e-mails as the writings of well-known comedian **Dennis Miller.** It was actually written by humorist, *Larry* **Miller,** in *The Weekly Standard.*

"The Palestinians want their own country. There's just one thing about that: There are no Palestinians. It's a made up word. Israel was called Palestine for two thousand years. Like 'Wiccan,' 'Palestinian' sounds ancient but is really a modern invention.

"Before the Israelis won the land in war, Gaza was owned by Egypt, and there were no 'Palestinians' then, and the West Bank was owned by Jordan, and there were no 'Palestinians' then. As soon as the Jews took over and started growing oranges as big as basketballs, what do you know, say hello to the 'Palestinians,' weeping for their deep bond with their lost 'land' and 'nation.'

"So for the sake of honesty, let's not use the word 'Palestinian' anymore to describe these delightful folks, who dance for joy at our deaths until someone points out they're being taped. Instead, let's call them what they are: 'Other Arabs From The Same General Area Who Are In Deep Denial About Never Being Able To Accomplish Anything In Life And Would Rather Wrap Themselves In The Seductive Melodrama Of Eternal Struggle And Death.' I know that's a bit unwieldy to expect to see on CNN. How about this, then: 'Adjacent Jew-Haters.'"

WHY THE PALESTINIAN PROBLEM WAS CAUSED BY THEIR OWN LEADERS *Jews and Power* is a provocative book written by a professor of comparative religion at Harvard, **Ruth R. Wisse**. "In denying the partition of Palestine, Arab governments also refused to allow the resettlement of the Palestinians, so that they could create perpetual evidence of Jewish iniquity.... Israel could be charged for the suffering of Palestinians only as long as their suffering could be sustained.... Palestinians Arabs are to be pitied...doubly unfortunate because theirs is the only displacement that is prolonged for political advantage...Israel did everything to absorb [them]."

Does Israel want to kill Palestinians? **Jonah Goldberg,** writing in the *National Review,* pointed out that during combat, "if the Israelis wanted to wipe out as many Palestinians as possible, they probably wouldn't issue warning to Gazans (by phone and leaflet) to get out of harm's way.... Like Israel, Gazans also have bomb shelters. So why don't they use them? They just reserve them for Hamas leaders and fighters. Better that those tunnels were used as shelters for civilians, but that would mean not letting them die for 'the greater good.'"

⸙ ✡ ⸙

KVELL TIME

FAMOUS STATEMENT BY MARK TWAIN ABOUT JEWS "If the statistics are right, the Jews constitute but one percent of the human race. It suggests a nebulous dim puff of stardust lost in the blaze of the Milky Way. Properly the Jew ought hardly to be heard of, but he is heard of, has always been heard of. He is as prominent on the planet as any other people, and his commercial importance is extravagantly out of proportion to the smallness of his bulk. His contributions to the world's list of great names in literature, science, art, music, finance, medicine, and abstruse learning are also away out of proportion to the weakness of his numbers."

DAVID BEN GURION, ISRAEL'S FIRST PRIME MINISTER, TELLS "WHY I AM A JEW" This is attributed to **David Ben Gurion** and was adapted, updated, and translated by an Israeli, **Dan Sporn.**

"Our condition, in Israel, has never been better than it is now! Only the television and the media make people think that the end of the world is near. Only 65 years ago, Jews were brought to death like sheep to slaughter. NO country, NO army. Only 60 years ago, seven Arab countries declared war on little Israel, the Jewish State, just a few hours after it was established.

"Today we have a beautiful country, a powerful Army, a strong Airforce, an adequate Navy and a thriving high-tech industry. Intel, Microsoft, and IBM have all developed their businesses here. Our doctors have won important prizes.... Israel today is among the few powerful countries that have nuclear technology and capabilities. (We will never admit it, but everyone knows.)

"Yes, sometimes morale is down, so what? This is only because we are mourning the dead while they are celebrating spilled blood. And this is the reason we will win after all..... "I am a Jew."

THE MOST E-MAILED ARTICLE ABOUT ISRAEL'S AMAZING ACCOMPLISHMENTS A decade ago, a "diplomat" named **Daniel Bernard**, Ambassador from France to the UK, "privately" called Israel"that shitty little country." This wonderful response, excerpted below, titled "One Shitty Little Country," was penned by **Tom Gross** in the *National Review*.

"Israel, the 100th smallest country, with less than 1/1000th of the world's population, can lay claim to the following.

- The cell phone was developed in Israel...Most of the Windows NT and XP operating systems were developed by Microsoft-Israel. The Pentium MMX Chip technology was designed in Israel at Intel.

- Both the Pentium-4 microprocessor and the Centrino processor were entirely designed, developed and produced in Israel...Voice mail technology was developed in Israel....

- Israel has the highest ratio of university degrees..., produces more scientific papers per capita than any other nation... highest per capita rates of patents filed.... Outside the United States and Canada, Israel has the largest number of NASDAQ listed companies.

- Israel has the highest average living standards in the Middle East....Twenty-four percent of Israel's workforce holds university degrees...ranking third in the industrialized world, after the United States and Holland....

- Twelve percent hold advanced degrees. Israel is the only liberal democracy in the Middle East.... Relative to its population, Israel is the largest immigrant-absorbing nation on earth. Israel has the world's second-highest per capita rate of new books. Israel has more museums per capita than any other country."

FAMOUS COLUMNIST ANN LANDERS REPRINTS "AN ANSWER TO AN ANTI-SEMITE" Ann Landers, born Esther Pauline Friedman, had the largest circulation of any column in the world. This column, penned in 1981, and repeated in 2002 in the *Chicago Tribune,* reprinted and updated an item originally written by popular humorist **Sam Levenson.**

It's a free world. You don't have to like Jews if you don't want to, but if you are going to be an anti-Semite, you should be consistent and turn your back on the medical advances that Jews have made possible.

"I am talking about the vaccine for hepatitis discovered by **Baruch Blumberg,** the Wasserman test for syphilis developed by **August von Wasserman,** and the first effective drug to fight syphilis developed by **Paul Ehrlich. Bela Schick** developed the diagnostic skin test for diphtheria. Insulin would not have been discovered if **Oskar Minkowski** had not demonstrated the link between diabetes and the pancreas. "It was **Burrill Crohn** who identified the disease that bears his name. **Alfred Hess** discovered that vitamin C could cure scurvy. **Casimir Funk** was the first to use vitamin B to treat beriberi. **Jonas Salk** developed the first polio vaccine. Later, **Albert Sabin** developed the oral version.

"Humanitarianism requires that we offer these gifts to all people of the world, regardless of race, color or creed. So the anti-Semites who don't want to accept these gifts can go ahead and turn them down, but I'm warning you, you aren't going to feel so good."

(NOTE: Ann Landers' daughter, **Margo Howard**, who went to Brandeis, wrote a wonderful book about what happened afterward, titled *Eat, Drink, and Remarry: Confessions of a Serial Wife.* Available at amazon.com)

SOURCES

BOOKS

Ashton, Dianne. *Hanukkah In America: A History.* New York: New York University Press, 2013.

Bader, David M. *Haikus for Jews: For You, A Little Wisdom.* New York: Harmony Books, 1999.

Berk, Sally (editor). *The Big Little Book of Jewish Wit & Wisdom.* New York: Black Dog & Leventhal Publishers, Inc., 2000.

Blech, Rabbi Benjamin. *The Complete Idiot's Guide to Jewish History and Culture.* New York: Alpha Books, 1999.

Brown, Judy. *The Funniest Jokes from the World's Best Comedians.* New York: Barnes & Noble Books, 1998.

Bush, Lawrence. *Jewdayo: A Daily Blast of Knowledge and Pride.* Accord, New York: Jewish Currents, 2012.

Cader Books. *That's Really Funny!* Kansas City, MO: Andrews McMeel Publishing, 2001.

Crystal, Billy. *700 Sundays.* New York: Grand Central Publishing, 2006.

Davis, Kenneth C. *Don't Know Much About the Bible.* New York: Avon Books, Inc., 1998.

Dundy, Elaine. *Elvis and Gladys.* New York: Dell Publishing Co., Inc., 1985.

Eisen, Armand. *Oy Vey! The Things They Say!* Kansas City, MO: Andrews and McMeel, A Universal Press Syndicate Company, 1994.

Falcon, Rabbi Ted, Ph.D. *Judaism for Dummies.* New York: Hungry Minds, Inc., 2001.

Goldstein, Jonathan & Wallace, Max. *Schmelvis: In Search of Elvis Presley's Jewish Roots.* Toronto, Ontario, Canada: ECW Press, 2002.

Jacobs, A. J. *The Year of Living Biblically.* New York: Simon & Schuster, 2008.

Katz, Molly. *Jewish As A Second Language.* New York: Workman Publishing, 1991.

Kolatch, Alfred J. *The Jewish Book of Why.* Middle Village, NY:

Jonathan David Publishers, Inc., 1981, 1995, 2000.

Klug, Lisa Alcalay. *Cool Jew: the Ultimate Guide for Every Member of the Tribe*. Kansas City, MO: Andrews McMeel Publishing, LLC, 2008.

Klug, Lisa Alcalay. *Hot Mamalah: The Ultimate Guide for Every Woman of the Tribe*. Kansas City, MO: Andrews McMeel Publishing, LLC, 2012.

Levin, Michael. *Where There's Smoke, There's Salmon: The Book of Jewish Proverbs*. New York: Fall River Press, 2001, 2008.

Mason, Phil. *Napoleon's Hemorrhoids: And Other Small Events That Changed The World*. New York: Castle Books, 2013.

McDonald, William (editor). *The New York Times: The Obits, Annual 2012*. New York: Workman Publishing, 2011.

Minkoff, David. *Oy Vey: More!: the Ultimate Book of Jewish Jokes part 2* New York: Thomas Dunne Books, St. Martin's Press, New York, 2008.

Moline, Rabbi Jack. *Growing Up Jewish*. New York: Penguin Books, 1987.

Oppenheimer, Jerry. *Seinfeld: the Making of An American Icon*. New York: Harper Collins, 2002.

Pogrebin, Abigail. *Stars of David: Prominent Jews Talk About Being Jewish*. New York: Broadway Books, 2005.

Rosen, Marcella, with Kornhaber, David. *Tiny Dynamo: How One of the World's Smallest Countries Is Producing Some of our Most Important Inventions*. Untold News, 2012.

Rosten, Leo. *The Joys of Yiddish*. New York: McGraw-Hill, 1968.

Samberg, Joel. *The Jewish Book Of Lists*. Secaucus, NJ: A Citadel Press Book, published by Carol Publishing Group, 1998.

Schochet, Elijah Judah. *Animal Life In Jewish Tradition*. New York: KTAV Publishing House, Inc., 1984.

Schochet, Stephen. *Hollywood Stories: Short Entertaining Anecdotes About the Stars and Legends of the Movies*. Hollywood Stories, 2010.

Senor, Dan, and Singer, Saul. *Start-Up Nation: The Story of Israel's Economic Miracle*. New York: Twelve, Hachette Book Group, 2011.

Siegel, Richard. *The First Jewish Catalog: A Do-It-Yourself Kit.* New York: The Jewish Publication Society, 1965.

Smith, Ronald L. *The Comedy Quote Dictionary.* New York: Doubleday, 1992.

Sorcher, Leonard. *The Optimist Sees the Bagel, the Pessimist Sees the Hole: Life's Little Jewish Instruction Book.* New York: Pocket Books, 1996.

Spalding, Henry D. *Joys of Jewish Humor.* Middle Village, NY: Jonathan David Publishers, 1985.

Wallechinsky, David, and Wallace, Amy. *The Book of Lists: the '90's Edition.* New York: Little, Brown, 1993.

Weiner, Ellis & Davilman, Barbara. *The Big Jewish Book for Jews.* New York: A Plume Book, published by Penguin Group, 2010.

Westheimer, Dr. Ruth K., and Mark, Jonathan. *Heavenly Sex: Sexuality in the Jewish Tradition.* New York: The Continuum Publishing Company, 1995.

Westheimer, Dr. Ruth K., and Yagoda, Ben. *All In A Lifetime: An Autobiography.* New York: Grand Central Publishing, 1988.

Wisse, Ruth. *Jews and Power.* New York: Nextbook/ Schocken, 2007.

Wolfe, Marjorie Gottlieb. *Are Yentas, Kibitzers, & Tummlers Weapons of Mass Instruction? Yiddish Trivia.* Syosset, NY: Malka Publications, 2004.

Wolfe, Marjorie Gottlieb. *Yiddish for Dog & Cat Lovers.* Syosset, NY: Malka Publications, 2007.

Zalampas, Sherree Owens. *Adolf Hitler: A Psychological Interpretation of His Views on Architecture, Art, and Music.* New York: Popular Press, 1990.

MAGAZINES

Forbes, The Economist, Harvard Magazine, Mental Floss, New York Magazine, The Week, The Weekly Standard.

NEWSPAPERS

The Boston Globe, The Brooklyn Paper, The Chicago Tribune, The Los Angeles Times, The Miami Herald, The New York Daily News, The New York Post, The New York Times, The Sun-Sentinel, The Times of Israel, The Washington Post.

WEBSITES

11points.com
ABCNEWS.com
about.com
aish.com
algemeiner.com
all-creatures.org
amazon.com
aol.com/news
boombeat.com
brainyquote.com
buzzfeed.com
buzztorah.com
CafePress.com
celebzen.com
chabad.org
Contactmusic.com
Cooljew.com
DailyMail.co.uk
downtrend.com
Facebook.com
Funnyandjewish.com
globes-co.il
Grubstreet.com
Haaretz.com
haruth.com
heeb.com
HuffingtonPost.com
imdb.com
imgur.com
Israel21c.com
Israeli-t.com
Israellycool.com
israelnationalnews.com
Jewage.org
jewcy.com
Jewfaq.org
JewishHumorCentral.com
Jewinthecity.com
JewishJournal.com
Jewishmag.com
jewishornot.blogspot.com
JewishPress.com
Jewishthinker.org
jewishvirtuallibrary.org

Jewlarious.com
Jewnews.com
Jewornotjew.com
jewsnews.co.il
jonstewart.net
jpost.com
Jspacenews.com
jta.org
katzsdelicatessen.com
Kveller.com
mondoweiss.net
news.yahoo.com
nj.com
nocamels.com
Popjewish.com
Quora.com
Reuters.com
Salon.com
singlesassy.com
slate.com
star-k.org
Tabletmag.com
teamcoco.com
Telegraph.co.uk
TheAtlantic.com
thebigfatjewishwedding.com
theblaze.com
thedailybeast.com
thedailymeal.com
TheGuardian.com/uk
theJewishindependent.com
TheJewniverse.com
thewrap.com
thrillist.com
TimesofIsrael.com
tlvfaces.com
tzvee.blogspot.com
unitedwithisrael.com
virtualjerusalem.com
wiki.answers.com
YouTube.com
yourjewishnews.com
yiddishbookcenter.org

ADDITIONAL SOURCES

CHAPTER 1: WHO'S A JEW? WHO KNEW? coolJew.com, Jewage.com, *Jewish Book of Lists,* jewornotjew.com, jspacenews.com, popjewish.com, *The Boston Globe, The New York Post,* virtualjerusalem.com, Wikipedia.org

CHAPTER 2: THAT'S ENTERTAINMENT: MOVIES & THEIR STARS: celebzen.com, *Hollywood Stories...* jewage.com, jewornotjew.com, *Mental Floss,* timesofisrael.com, virtualjerusalem.com

CHAPTER 3: THAT'S ENTERTAINMENT—MORE CELEBS: imdb.com, jewishornot.blogspot.com, jewornotjew.com, jspacenews.com, Virtualjerusalem.com, *Wonder of Wonders*

CHAPTER 4: ROYALTY & POLITICIANS: *Forbes,* forward.com, israelnationalnews.com, Jewishpress.com, jta.org, Telegraph.co.uk, thejc.com, *The New York Times: The Obits,* TLVFaces.com, Wikipedia.org

CHAPTER 5: JEW-BILATION—MORE MEMBERS OF THE TRIBE: buzzfeed.com, *Jewdayo, The Book of Lists*

CHAPTER 7: JEWISH LIFE (& PETS): *Book of Lists,* forward.com, jewage.com, *Napoleon's Hemorrhoids,* teamcoco.com.

CHAPTER 8: SPORTS: aol.com/news, buzzfeed.com, jewage.com, mondoweiss.net, Wikipedia.org, yourjewishnews.com.

CHAPTER 9: HANUKKAH & CHRISTMAS: buzztorah.com, *Hanukkah in America.*

CHAPTER 10: PASSOVER: buzztorah.com, globes-co.il, slate.com.

CHAPTER 11: PRAYS WELL WITH OTHERS: *The Week.*

CHAPTER 12: NOSHING, OR KOSHER FOOD & WINE:

cooljew.com, forward.com, theatlantic.com Wikipedia.org

CHAPTER 13: YIDDISH & HEBREW: *Jews and Power*, jta.org via jewcy.com

CHAPTER 14: LIFE IN ISRAEL: NoCamels.com, *The New York Post,* timesofisrael.com

CH 15: SERIOUSLY: DEFENSE, PREJUDICE & THE THIRD REICH: brainyquote.com, israelnationalnews.com, jewishmag.com, jewnews.com, theatlantic.com, theblaze.com, Wikipedia.org, news.yahoo.com

CHAPTER 16: WORDS OF WISDOM: downtrend.com, haaretz.com, virtualjerusalem.com.

SUGGESTED ADDITIONAL READING/WATCHING/ LISTENING

RADIO & TV: www.jbstv.org (Jewish broadcasting service)

https://soundcloud.com/tablet-magazine This is Tablet's daily online magazine of Jewish news, ideas, and culture, and is also home to Vox Tablet podcast hosted by Sara Ivry.

FUNNY WEBSITES: www.heebmagazine.com; www.hipsterjew.com; www.haruth.com/jhumor, www.aish.com/j/jt, www.jewishhumorcentral.com (The author of this last site wrote a great book titled, *Israel is a Funny Country: Funniest Jewish Videos on the Internet.* At amazon.com.)

NEWSLETTER ABOUT ISRAEL: Subscribe to the daily news stories & interesting commentaries about Israel & the Middle East at www.centerpeace.org.

JEWISH BOOK SITES: www.jewishbookcouncil.org, www.jewishreviewofbooks.com, http//www.judaica.com/books.html www.yiddishbookcenter.org

ABOUT THE AUTHOR

Paulette Cooper (Noble) lives in Palm Beach with her husband, **Paul Noble**, and her two Imperial Toy Shih-Tzus, Polo and Peek-a-Boo.

She has written 23 books (and over 1,000 articles) on a variety of subjects: *The Scandal of Scientology, The Medical Detectives, 277 Secrets Your Dog Wants You To Know, 277 Secrets Your Cat Wants You To Know, Palm Beach Pets & The People Who Love Them, etc.*

She is the winner of eight writing awards, and according to Wikipedia, her books have sold over a half a million copies. She also writes a regular column in the *Palm Beach Daily News*.

A book about Paulette, written by **Tony Ortega**, is titled, *The Unbreakable Miss Lovely: How the Church of Scientology Tried To Destroy Paulette Cooper*. It is available at *amazon.com*.

Additional copies of *Was Elvis Jewish?...* are available at *waselvisjewish.com* and *polopublishing.com*.

See *www.paulettecooper.com* for more books by Paulette. To reach her, e-mail PauletteC@aol.com.

ABOUT THE EDITOR

Paul Noble is a retired TV programming executive for Lifetime, Metromedia and Fox. He serves on the Board of The Palm Beach County Film & Television Commission. He has won five Emmys and has produced many major television talk shows. He also takes the photographs for Paulette's column in the *Palm Beach Daily News*. He is co-President of the Circumnavigators Club with his wife, Paulette. He graduated from Cornell and has a Masters from Boston University. *www.PaulRNoble.com*

www.ingramcontent.com/pod-product-compliance
Lightning Source LLC
Chambersburg PA
CBHW070800100426
42742CB00012B/2205